How to hypnotise chooks

How to hypnotise chooks

and other great yarns

MAX WALKER

Publications

Garry Sparke and Associates
P.O. Box 360, Glen Waverley, Victoria 3150

First published 1987
© Max Walker.

Typeset by GS Typesetting
Printed by Magenta Press.
40 Geddes St., Mulgrave.

ISBN 0 908081 51 0

INTRODUCTION

When my cricket career finished midway through the 1981/82 season, the structure of my life changed dramatically. So much so that today, no longer am I an architect or a professional cricketer, in fact it's difficult to get into two words an appropriate title. Whatever the title, one thing is certain — I lead a great, erratic and at times fascinating existence, and I really do enjoy sharing views and ideas and experiences.

Today my commitments involve TV and radio, an enormous amount of travelling to various speaking engagements writing and the occasional corporate video and the odd TV commercial. And quite a few other things as well too . . . like this book!

I love people and I'm lucky enough to be able to meet a huge cross-section of the community, most of whom have shown so much wonderful hospitality to me that it would be impossible to reciprocate. I thank them very much for letting me share some of their time and their thoughts.

Even as a kid I seemed to be surrounded by lots of different people. I only have to look back to my early days in Tassie, when I lived in the Empire Hotel, North Hobart, a good industrial beer drinking pub. There seemed to be an endless supply of my dad's mates and his stories, always rich in color and chock full of incredible characters. We used to be spellbound by the never ending exaggeration and humour.

All those colourful characters parading through the pub gave me a different insight into some of the pleasant and not so pleasant aspects of life. It was certainly different to the formal education gained at school. I think above all it allowed me to laugh a lot . . . even today I still laugh a lot because laughter is a beautiful tonic.

Also the customers of the Empire Hotel provided the most unusual and endless supply of backyard bowlers that any young man with aspirations to Test match greatness could possibly want. By 6 o'clock most afternoons, none of them lacked any confidence at all. A bit like Bay 13 or The Hill in Sydney, eh?

My dad, known as 'Big Max' — who always told a good story, continually encouraged me to see the lighter side of life; it's been a great philosophy. He almost certainly must be responsible for my joy of practical jokes.

And that's the theme of this book, lots of tales, lots of jokes, all drawn from 39 wonderful years, and guaranteed to provoke a giggle or two.

MAX WALKER

Dedication

I wish to dedicate this book to all those wonderful characters that have enabled me to look at life's many situations with a smile and maybe just a touch of tongue in cheek . . . this is your book.

CONTENTS

Chapter One

THIS WAS SERIOUS . . . SO I LAUGHED A LOT

The more my stick of chalk came to the tip of its beak, the more cross-eyed it became.

Learning to Hypnotise Chooks
'HE WAS HAVING A LOT OF TROUBLE TRYING TO STAY ON THE PERCH'

When it comes to eating I guess I'm not too bad on the old fang. But after eating chicken for dinner at the last 17 straight speaking engagements — I've finally had enough.

Don't get me wrong, I still like chook a bit but I can now understand how Keith Stackpole, the former Australian opening batsman, built up a strong dislike for eating chicken while in the Caribbean during the 1973 Australian cricket tour of the West Indies.

During that tour we ate chicken, or should I say very, very wild water fowl morning, noon and night, with the odd variation being curried goat, fried rice and 23 different varieties of 'blow flies'.

Actually the color of the chicken meat served up to us varied from white, as it should be, to a sickly looking brown to a greyish tone, camouflaged with a different type of gravy each meal. My goodness some of those water birds were tough, too!

At one evening meal in Guyana I can vividly remember Dougie Walters attacking a very brownish 'drumstick' with a serrated-edged knife — it literally ricocheted off the flesh and bounced back towards him. He traded his chicken meal for something a little more palatable and definitely easier to eat —tomato soup!

I seem to have been plagued by these feathered 'friends' all my life —and I suppose the odd first ball 'duck' too! Even as a kid, they used to cause more than their fair share of trouble!

I think I was about 14 at the time, on a Saturday the week before Easter. Halfway through the afternoon Dad was serving in the bar of the Tasmanian pub he owned when this character came in, walked straight up to the old man and asked him if he'd care to buy half a dozen fresh chooks.

"How much?" asked Dad. Five bob was the reply.

"Are you sure they're fresh?" Dad followed up, with more than a passing amount of interest. Even in those days five bob was a pretty good price for fresh poultry.

The chap immediately produced a flour sack on the bar and proffered the birds for inspection. They were fresh, right enough. In fact they were barely cold.

Dad examined each one critically, hefting them to test their weight, pinching their tails for plumpness, and flexing their breastbones to gauge their age. Each apparently passed this professional judgment satisfactorily because Dad made a counter offer.

"Give you four and sixpence," he said.

"Make it four and ninepence."

"Done," said my old man who went to the till, counted out one pound, eight shillings and sixpence, gave it to the bloke (who immediately bought half a dozen bottles and left) and took the chooks through to the kitchen and gave them to the cook.

Shortly afterwards a couple of customers came back from the toilet with a most unusual complaint. "Max," they said to Dad, "you'd better get out the back — your toilets are blocked."

When we went out to investigate, a quite astounding sight greeted us. The place was covered in entrails, heads and feathers from wall to wall. It didn't take much figuring out to realise that the recently departed poultry purveyor had killed, cleaned and plucked the beasts in the gents.

This prompted Dad to make a hasty visit to the kitchen and warn the cook that perhaps he should take a little extra care when washing the birds.

All of this was bad enough — I was given the job of cleaning up the mess —but the punchline came at about six o'clock next morning when the yardman banged on Dad's door.

"Hey, Max," he said, "you'd better get down to the chookyard. Six of yer best layers are missing."

Dad was about the only bloke who didn't enjoy his Easter dinner!

After replacing the six missing hens I used one of the new ones for an unusual experiment —I'd read somewhere that chooks were very easy to hypnotise . . . so I followed the instructions very closely. The hard part was catching one. When I entered the fowl-yard I was viewed as an unwelcome intruder! Nevertheless, I soon snatched a black one from behind, grabbed it by the legs and immediately turned the unlucky bird over and placed it on its back.

As suggested, I began to drag a piece of chalk across the abrasive concrete path surface which was now supporting the upturned chooks head.

The closer my stick of chalk came to the tip of its beak the more cross-eyed it became until finally the chalk stopped hard up against the bewildered bird's head. Success, one hypnotised fowl.

I stood back a pace to admire my effort in rendering the laying bird motionless when Paddy my pedigree boxer dog swooped on the poor unfortunate thing. And, with barely the bright red crown showing from the corner of the dog's mouth, my pet made off with my subject.

Unfortunately for the squawking chook it took me several minutes to track my dog down . . . there he was, glint in his eye, feathers hanging out of his mouth like a red-indian chief's head-dress!

Paddy had himself and the chook jammed into a tight little space hard up against the back fence and between the fowl-house. Yes, my fine feathered friend had been plucked from the eyeballs down to the nape of its neck, and it wasn't liking it either. Well you couldn't blame it.

To this day I still don't know how to snap a chook out from under its hypnotic spell. My friendly canine pet had achieved that end for me without even knowing it. It really was a pathetic sight to see this strange, half-strangled red neck stagger across the fowl-yard to rejoin his mates.

At that stage he was having a lot of trouble staying on the perch, so, the obvious happened! He ended up on the meal table of the Walker household that night.

As for my dog, well . . . he'd got a taste for the feathered variety.

Even without drawing any blood the beautifully proportioned four legged animal enjoyed what he did.

This first encounter perhaps was the reason for several future escapades by Paddy, the chooks' friend. After all, they are such a playful breed of dog . . . the more reaction to their playing, the more they want to play. Our cook could vouch for that every time she put out the rubbish!

The last straw came about 12 months later when the neighboring veterinary surgeon lobbed in the hotel foyer demanding to see Dad.

"Your dog's just killed 14 of my chooks . . . and, what are you going to do about it?" he said rather gruffly.

Dad said, "It couldn't be our dog because he's in our backyard . . . anyway he wouldn't do that sort of thing!" I knew better — he was my dog!

"You want proof?" demanded the red-faced vet. "Yes," said my old man rather smugly.

Well you should have seen it! There he was, my beautiful tan boxer dog being dragged bodily through the front door of the pub by his silver studded collar, head at 45 degrees to the vertical but looking ever so pleased with himself. The tell-tale signs were sticking to the saliva dribbling from his mouth. He must have had 50 feathers stuffed in his choppers!

Paddy had climbed the metal fire escape stairs and up a 30 degree inclined corrugated iron roof to the ridge.

Then he must have dug in his toe-nails on the way down the other side . . . then crashed into the box guttering and parapet wall. He must have plucked up enough courage to leap five metres into a yard full of hens —with catastrophic results.

My Dad had to buy 14 fully feathered squawking hens and unfortunately Paddy my mate got a rest on a country property.

Reading, 'Riting and the Cuts

'HER AIM WAS PERFECT. WHACK! WHACK! WHACK!

Can you remember getting the cuts at school? Gee, I certainly can. Those were the days when a classroom consisted of a rectangular-shaped room, with a blackboard at the front. No open planned study areas, calculators, television monitors or computers.

Chalk and the blackboard were used for instruction. Reading, 'Riting and 'Rithmetic they called it —the 3R's.

Discipline was basic too! If you did the wrong thing then you got into

11

Really it wasn't even a challenge. I pretended to be helpful by . . . picking up a piece of wayward chalk.

trouble. For a minor misdemeanor the teacher in charge got to dish out the punishment, but for a serious offence it was a rendezvous with the headmaster.

I doubt if anyone could go through a decent education eystem without getting into strife sooner or later.

In my case it was pretty often I guess, but then again I have never professed to be an angel . . .

My first taste of the cane was delivered by a tottery, little old lady named 'Old Ma Hughes'. She must have been 90 at the time.

In many ways she was an unforgettable character . . . deep lines of experience were etched into her face. Dangling from her witch-like chin were five or six strands of silver hair — the subject of much sarcastic back-chatting from her students.

I'd run foul of the old lady because ego got the better of me, when I accepted a challenge to place one or two 'stink bombs' in the old lady's hair, while she was writing on the blackboard.

Stink bombs, as we called them, were created from biting the tiny seeds from one of Tasmania's native flowers and depositing a fair lathering of saliva on the gaping flesh. The result was a vulgar rotten-egg smell.

Really it wasn't even a challenge. I pretended to be helpful by creeping up behind the skinny and fragile little teacher, picking up a piece of wayward chalk from the bare timber floor boards and quickly placing the 'bomb' in her hairnet, before handing over the chalk.

It was a great laugh for a while . . . until she could stand the odor no more! In fact she discreetly asked if anyone was having trouble with flatulence, but nobody knew what the strange word meant.

The back row of the classroom of which I was a member, couldn't help themselves, and burst into loud laughter. At the same time the teacher's pet, named Annette (butter wouldn't melt in her mouth), dobbed us in . . . and me in particular.

Well, time for the cane. The little old lady was blue in the face after standing on a stool to reach the 'old faithful' willowy piece of branch hidden carefully on top of the hardwood cupboard, near the stage. To say the teacher was upset would have been an understatement.

"Hand out Walker!" she shouted.

She then launched herself off the 300 mm high platform with all her might . . . her aim was perfect. Whack! Whack! Whack! Whack! Four of the best in quick succession. There was a stunned silence in the classroom as I struggled to hold back my feelings.

I didn't plant stink bombs in her hair ever again.

But I did put a frog in Annette's ink well. The frog jumped out of the well and on to the horrid little girl's transcription book. I received four more cuts for my troubles.

I was a bit of a lad with the marbles early on too — a real dead-eye dick!

I always had several pockets full of marbles with me at school — they eventually became my undoing.

It just seemed natural to want to continually play with them but the familiar noise of marbles bouncing on the floorboards irritated Old Ma Hughes — with the expected result.

I don't know what it was but I seemed to be attracted to that frightening piece of equipment that lived on top of the storage cupboard in Old Ma Hughes' classroom.

Before my fourth year was completed I managed to feel the biting pain of that big stick a few more times . . . yes, fourth grade was a bad year for yours truly!

I even got caught nicking out of the classroom 15 minutes before school finished, so that I could get to football practice early. I had several hundred lines to write and missed football practice altogether!

By the time I was in grade six, I pretty much knew what to expect, when I managed to get on the wrong side of a teacher.

The big question was . . . whether to risk placing an exercise book into the bum of your trousers, just in case the headmaster said, "bend over son"?

Then there was the myth about rubbing orange peel on the palms of one's hands. The intention being that the orange-skin moisture would make the cane slide quickly off an outstretched hand. It doesn't work.

There was always the rigid hand versus the limp fingered approach — both of these hurt a lot!

But not as much as having the back of your hand placed on the desk top . . . then whack! That was the worst — a bit like getting your hand stapled to a bench top with a hydraulic press!

Some of the masters or teachers I met under these difficult circumstances, had a definite mean streak in their nature — they never used to aim at the numb and calloused upturned hand! Much more painful was a direct hit to the knuckle area of the base of the thumb.

One of these discipline sticks even had a name — 'Excalibur' just like the mythological sword of King Arthur. It belonged to Mr Wilfred Asten, deputy head master of the Friends' School in Hobart. My chance meeting with Excalibur was as usual self-inflicted and deserved.

My only crime really was to be a good hooker of the short-pitched delivery at cricket practice . . . high over the fence adjoining our practice nets and into the apple orchard next door.

When you're a growing boy there's nothing quite like a good feed of fresh apples from a nearby orchard, is there?

The biggest problem for me was that I'd hit the ball, so I had to go and fetch it. Unfortunately, I took my time getting back — the owner of the property sprung me. Teeth deeply sunk into a beautiful ripe Jonathan, juice trickling from the corners of my mouth, I couldn't have been happier, until I saw this irritable old man coming after me with a broom handle.

I managed to scale the paling fence without copping too many bruises . . . but much verbal abuse was being poured at me. So I replied!

The ageing orchardist reported me to the headmaster, and his deputy had me standing outside his office door quick smart before the bell rang at nine o'clock next morning.

Yes, I was guilty, but dead set unlucky — we'd been pinching those apples for years! Why now?

Nevertheless the time was very near for me to meet Excalibur . . . I had heard so much about the dimensions of this magnificent piece of cane, that I didn't really fancy the scene at all! Nor the hurt.

Soon Mr. Asten explained how I'd crossed the thin white line that separates right from wrong. Then he introduced me to his friend Excalibur.

My life seemed to race past my eyes at a million miles an hour, as I stemmed back a well of tears, until I got outside in the dark, smelly, highly polished corridor.

Quickly I headed for the ablutions block to check out the damage and dry off the pain expressing itself in front of my eye-balls — didn't need the other kids to see me like this. They'd call me a sheila if I cried.

Nothing wrong with crying after six of the best deliveries I've ever faced in my life . . . including those from the West Indians.

The Tractor and the Water Skis

'HIS TROUSERS JUST PEELED OFF HIM, NO TROUBLE AT ALL'

When my Dad did his apprenticeship to the building trade, he did so under the watchful eye of a master builder named Tom Lipscombe, one of the most successful builders operating in Hobart during the mid '40s.

In those days, one young apprentice was to work with every two tradesmen, and they were not allowed to smoke or drink . . . how things have changed! Another fascinating discipline was that the young apprentice was not allowed to contract into an early marriage under the bond.

These young men were in turn educated in business as well as the trade itself and became in fact part of the master's family.

The master was bound by law to teach the trade properly and especially to watch over the morals of the boys in his charge . . . it must have worked okay in the case of my old man because it didn't take him long before he became a fully-fledged master builder himself.

Employing staff and apprentices is often a gamble — and Dad had a few losses.

One was Herbie a licensed drainer and a mental giant who was to complete all the draining work on a very nice executive type house to be built in the then expanding suburb of Berriedale on the banks of the beautiful Derwent River, not far from the famous Cadbury's chocolate factory.

Digging trenches and laying pipes was definitely Herbie's job. But on one fateful day during early construction work on this dwelling, things didn't quite work out for poor old Herb who, by the way, didn't have a driver's licence.

Herb was left on his own after lunch to finish off a couple of the trenches, but someone had parked our old fashioned, yellow Caterpillar tractor right in line with the direction of Herb's diggings — so he had a problem.

I'll give the muscle-bound drainer his dues because he walked straight round to the front of the tractor grille to crank start the engine. He was successful after just a few tugs on the lever, and the engine began to purr loudly but without any apparent rhythm. It sounded 'sick'.

So Herb jumped up on to the metal seat, experimented with the badly worn clutch and the squeaky brake pedal and, much to his astonishment the rusty old contraption took off with a start, but he didn't know how to stop either the engine, or the rapid movement forward . . . which was quickly getting out of control.

It appeared Herb had three main options. Firstly he could follow the unmade dirt track leading back on to the main highway — no way, too much traffic and after all he could have been booked for unlicensed driving and obstructing traffic.

Then of course there was always the Derwent River but Herb couldn't swim either.

Thirdly he could have driven the tractor into the adjacent neighbor's property and completely wrecked several much loved gardens.

He'd already up-ended the rusty, primitive, corrugated iron dunny which was merely protecting the sacred hole in the ground from the elements. What was he going to say to the boss? Nothing unless he could get off the tractor!

Yes our beloved drainer stayed on that tractor for a further hour and a half, until the machine ran out of petrol. It wasn't exactly the Indianapolis 500 or the Adelaide Grand Prix but he did get very giddy after about 500 laps of the building site.

Meanwhile my father 'Big Max', and myself then answering to 'Little Max', were enjoying some aquatic adventures. The owner of the proposed house, Charlie, had a snappy little runabout with a growling Mercury outboard motor.

Both Dad and myself accepted the generous lunchtime offer of some free water skiing even though neither of us had tackled the sport before.

Big Max didn't look at all comfortable in the murky water — maybe that was because the trouser legs of his builders' overalls were billowing out like a spacesuit after they'd trapped quite substantial pockets of air below the water level.

Dad wouldn't admit that he couldn't ski, especially after he'd told Charlie it would be a breeze. A costly error of judgement.

I dare not think how much water my Dad swallowed just trying to put both skis on — but it was a lot!

All set to go, the nylon cord was soon taut, the engine roared but the nose of the fibreglass boat pointed to the sky in disgust . . . it could not budge my old man . . . he was firmly entrenched in the soft muddy river bed. In fact the 17 stone mass of my father was just too much for the skis. The louder the boat's throttle revved, the more he laughed. And the more he laughed, his aching arms and legs just kept sinking lower into the water until, finally I reckon the two water skis must have been buried at least a metre into the slush on the river bed.

Now only his cheeky face sparkled above the calm water's surface. He was still laughing at the whole scene as the bib of his overalls extended pregnantly in front of him, when quite unexpectedly — success!

My dad's massive frame lurched forward out of the water, head long towards the small craft like a dolphin — he was hanging on for grim death. Behind him appeared a beautiful white V-shaped wake; he was still on his belly and obviously had no skis —the force of the extra revs had dragged him right out of his mud encased rubber ski-shoes.

But the sheer weight of water rushing into his large air-filled overalls

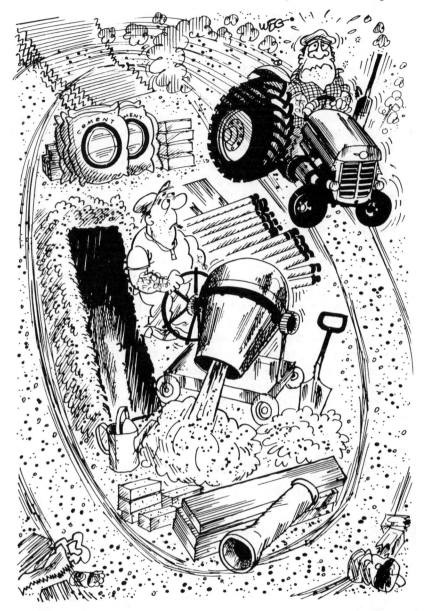

He did get very giddy after about 500 laps of the building site.

snapped the two straps supporting his bib and without any problem at all his trousers just peeled off him. He looked like a prostrate superman speeding over the smooth water's surface.

By the time he'd stopped charging through the water, he was half way across the Derwent river . . . bobbing up and down like a huge white sperm whale, shining under the midday sun.

17

It was a slow trip back to shore as we had to find and retrieve my old man's various pieces of clothing, as well as the two skis buried somewhere in the churned up cloudy water.

Meanwhile, back at the building site, things were looking a lot better for Herb.

Barry the young apprentice had finally arrived back from his lunch break just before the boss and myself did, and of course the tractor had eventually stopped dead after running out of fuel.

But some five cubic yards of concrete had arrived ready to pour into the staircases and some ramps. And the object of any concrete pour is to get it into position as quickly as possible.

In those days, concrete delivery was by means of a flat tray truck — no revolving agitators and pumps that are standard in today's concrete trucks.

Now Barry, who was also a mental heavyweight, placed himself in line with proceedings while Dad and Herbie continued to belt the top of the tilted tray with pieces of timber to free the load. Finally it happened — the whole lot gave way with a gush and partly buried poor Barry.

It took three men quite a while to frantically dig Bazza out of his concrete boots . . . no mafia on site either!!

And to top off a great first three months work for Mr Walker, Master Builder, Barry later managed to saw himself off a roof rafter.

The resultant 20 feet fall didn't do any further brain damage to that already present, but he did break out his hand-saw and sprain his ankle.

Novice apprentice Barry never did get to complete his time, he was too big a risk, not only to himself, but everyone else on the job.

Dying for a Laugh
'THE FIRST YEAR BOYS USED TO GET PUT IN THE COFFIN'

Recently I was reading a newspaper and the headline stated, 'Mourners sent home as coffin jammed in grave.' The article reminded me of a couple of stories my Dad — Max Walker senior — used to often tell. As always he embellished the truth to make them even more interesting . . . well as interesting as a story about coffins can get, without being offensive to someone.

You see, as a young man he was learning his trade as a carpenter and joiner under the watchful eye of one Mr Tom Lipscombe, one of the largest and most successful builders in Hobart of the time. One of his company's lesser contracts was to supply local funeral parlors with all of their coffins, depending on the demand.

In those days the basic coffin was constructed from the now precious timber, Huon pine, about 1¼ inches thick. The shoulders were bent with a saw-cut and glued while the bottom was made from banana cases and a

18

sheet of waterproof sisal paper — much better than today's supermarket version!

Once enough of these sombre capsules were completed they'd be piled onto a lorry about six of them high, by 10 coffins long, and then delivered to the undertaker.

I believe on one occasion Mr Lipscombe's company ran foul of the health department because the naked truck-load of coffins was not covered from public view by a tarpaulin — how terrible! Once your dead you're dead, and all the germs or contamination in the world aren't going to make an ounce of difference. But if you're alive . . . well that's a different matter as I'll describe.

As is the case with most apprentices, there is always an initiation ceremony — the first year boys used to get put in a coffin, and the lid nailed down.

One day while the boss was out, a startled young man named Timothy underwent the ordeal. He seemed to fit snugly into the unlined coffin, according to my old man. The lid was then tightly nailed down amidst some very abusive language — I couldn't blame him!

After approximately half an hour of carrying the poor guy around the workshop on timber studs, mocking pall bearers and mourners, the boss unexpectedly arrived back at work to see this weird ritual going on.

"What are you blokes doing there?" he said.

"Picking it up to see if it's balanced sir!" came the reply in unison.

"Where's Timothy?" asked Mr Lipscombe. "Gone to the shop to get his lunch, sir!" the mischievous woodworkers shouted, in order to muffle Tim's protestations.

No sooner had the bossman disappeared down the stairs than the coffin was placed on the dirty timber floor of the carpenter's workshop to continue the initiation. Heaps of shavings and blocks were quickly shovelled on to it as if falling dirt was filling up a grave-site.

Meanwhile my 'father-to-be' began reciting the last rites on the poor fellow: " . . On the green hills far away . . . may he rest in peace . . . for thine is the Kingdom, the power and the glory, for ever and ever, Amen. God rest his soul!"

Again another stifled shout for help! Timothy had now been in the coffin for almost $1\frac{1}{2}$ hours — poor lad!!!

Finally the bullies let the terrified apprentice out of the coffin . . . it was like a jack in a box. He leapt out of the pine masterpiece and raced down the stairs screaming about a lot of mad fellows upstairs and adamant that he would definitely not be coming back!

My old man suggested it did take a long time before he came back to work.

Then there was a real funeral — a dear friend of my Dad's.

As the four impeccably dressed pall bearers carried the beautifully finished, ornate coffin from the church to the waiting hearse, the bottom half of the coffin sub-stratum pulled away from the upper coffin . . . remember today the bases are only made of a compacted fibreboard, and fixed by staples to the upper section of the box.

Two of the quick thinking pall bearers shoved the dead man's legs and coffin base back to where it ought to have been — saving an awkward situation, but that was only temporary.

On the walk from the hearse to the cut in the ground at the cemetery, the other half of the sub-strata opened up. Nevertheless the funeral proceeded, placing the coffin over the burial site in the usual manner.

Worse was to come. As the ledges were removed and the coffin lowered into the badly dug grave, it jammed, so the ropes were loosened from the under-side of the coffin.

The priest suggested to one of the grave-diggers that maybe a gentle tap on the offending coffin corner would work. As you can imagine the results were nothing short of catastrophic.

The grave-digger feared the lid might move and open up but no one could have predicted the body falling out of the bottom and resting on the grave floor.

It was a terrible ordeal for the mourners to witness and embarrassing for the priest who promptly told everyone to leave the area while some very hasty repairs were done and the poor fellow resurrected back into the coffin.

Needless to say more research and modern technology are needed in coffin construction! I only hope when I visit the great MCG in the sky that the silly so and so making my coffin gets enough staples into the sub strata. Because by then I could be a big boy — well I'm a big boy now, but wait 'til I grow up!

Maybe I should put my architectural skills to work and design a decent coffin with a damp-proof concrete slab floor and cedar-lined internal walls and a solar-panelled lid. The mind boggles.

Suffering for the Sport
'MY GOSH, I THOUGHT . . . OR SOMETHING A LITTLE STRONGER!'

Looking back on a career almost totally committed to sport, it would be fair to say that pain and I are friends. Anyone contemplating a long and successful career in sport would realise that self hurt and injuries are part of the process, but as a young kid I realised that the sight of blood was not going to impress me.

I had a nasty experience with blood and it wasn't even my own blood — it was my dog's!

On my 12th birthday I was presented with a golden-tanned boxer pup

—he was just beautiful. A more playful and cuddly pup I could never have wished for.

One fateful Sunday afternoon two years later in the backyard of my Dad's Empire Hotel, Paddy the boxer dog and I began a mock fight. The dog would grab me by the hand or wrist as I attempted to pat him on the head or on the point of his very square nose. My canine friend was continually backing away to make room for his next assault.

Unfortunately for Paddy he took one step back too many. The outcome was a nasty one — a huge, spiked cactus became embedded deep in the dog's rear end. Needless to say my hairy friend let out an ear-piercing yelp. Who would blame him? A gash about 75mm long and maybe 120mm deep. Not a pretty sight.

Just how deep was difficult to tell initially because Paddy refused to keep still — in fact I'm sure he made himself giddy by continually chasing his short, stubby tail, in an effort to lick the wound clean.

A short time later, just around the corner from the pub, in the local vet's surgery, I was consoling my dog who was now almost two years old and a far cry from the two-month-old puppy I used to know.

Just imagine the dog standing quietly, but in pain, on a yellow laminex table top, and not without some difficulty. His toenails didn't seem to grip the shiny surface and his legs continually spread towards the table edges. My arm was firmly wrapped around Paddy's neck; saliva from his not so pretty mouth splashed on the table surface.

By design I was looking away from the rear end where all the action was taking place. All I could see was the stumpy tail wiggling anxiously as the veterinary surgeon named Ralph examined the damage to my pet's hindquarters.

Obviously a painkilling injection was being given because every muscle in the dog's body tensed and the whimpering increased. At this stage I was coping, but not as well as Paddy.

My problems began when the vet's latex-gloved fingers began to squeeze as much blood as they could from the wound. It didn't look too flash collecting on the table top. As the clots formed an almost artistic image, my mind was beginning to fade quickly.

Yes, the room began to spin around and I let go of my proud boxer dog. Ralph the vet took a great diving catch to his left, grabbing my crumpled body just inches from the floor.

I sat with my head between my legs in a corner as Ralph continued his work. Five stitches were needed to close the gaping hole.

I remained in the vet's surgery for 30 mins. or so while the dog courageously strolled home!

Fifteen months later at school football practice I experienced the sight of my own blood being spilt.

As could be expected in Tasmania the weather was bleak — about four deg. C. and raining cats and dogs. It was so bad on some nights that a couple of our less courageous players used to run the three warm-up laps in plastic raincoats so as not to get wet. They never did make it into the first 18.

The football was always hard to handle in the wet, at times it would become soggy and slippery like soap — not much fun.

In attempting an overhead mark I paid the ultimate penalty. A striking pain from the top of my head to the extremity of my left hand. Maybe I had put a finger out of joint? I grabbed my left hand to my muddy chest, it was ringing like a set of church bells . . . this was real pain!

Apart from a stress fracture to the same wrist, I had never suffered pain like this before . . . well maybe at the hands of a dentist . . . but this time it was in my hand and not in my mouth.

I peeled open the four fingers from the palm of my left hand to reveal a handful of blood. My gosh, I thought . . . or something a little stronger!

The hand basin in the dressing room was soon filled with blood in an effort to clean the cut. But it wasn't just a cut, I had split the webbing of my hand between the index and second fingers. I was almost physically sick as I looked straight through the palm of my hand to the dirty, concrete floor below. I knew then that I wasn't going to get away with this little injury without undergoing a lot more pain.

Soon I was sitting in the outpatients department of the Royal Hobart Hospital with my coach Robert Carr. We did what everyone else did for the next two hours — gazed at the ceiling and picked faults with everyone else who also had to kill time. Boring for a kid.

By about 8 o'clock on that freezing night, a trifle blue in color, I exploded — "where's all the bloody doctors!" (I could even say that at 15).

After that outburst, I sat in silence for another hour inside a small cubicle with the white cotton curtain draped across the entrance. I'd almost forgotten what I was doing there when I heard echoing footsteps getting louder. It had to be my turn.

I must have got a first night intern because he told me what I already knew. "You've got a bit of split webbing sonny!" At this stage I almost felt like saying, "You're joking aren't you?" But common sense prevailed. The young doctor was only trying to help. It's just that he'd been a bit slow and there's nothing quite like queuing up to get a split webbing fixed on a cold winter's night in Hobart.

Then his assistant-cum-nurse arrived. Even at 15 I could tell she was worth 8 out of 10 — well in uniform anyway. Blonde 36-24-36, she looked good enough to me. She could have made me to do anything for her . . . except open my fingers!

After holding them tightly together for almost four hours what did she expect? A miracle! I was sure whoever got to open my fingers was going to inflict a serious amount of pain on my body. I was right!

After much persuasion, the split webbing lay exposed on the side table on the top of a very clinical white cloth. In the stainless steel tray adjacent were a lot of dangerous looking weapons with either points or a cutting edge. Right in the middle was a huge needle . . . it must have been eight inches long. Gee it was big!

While the nurse prepared the wound for stage two of the exercise I couldn't help thinking how much that bloody big needle might hurt. I had become obsessed with this instrument of pain but I guess I wasn't the first person ever to fear a needle.

The doctor was very clever because he loaded the needle behind his back so that I couldn't see the full dimension of the pain killer. Killer would have been a more appropriate term!

He about turned 180 deg. towards me with a very plastic smile and a sadistic glint in his eye. The enormous needle was pointed at the fluorescent light on the ceiling, cocked between his thumb and forefingers, ready for action.

The next 10 seconds seemed like eternity as he took aim at my pink and purple hand. Helen, the nurse, supported my wrist above the table with one hand and separated my fingers with the other. Her touch was almost sensuous for a fleeting moment, until the needle punctured my skin. Firstly on the back of my hand, just above the index finger knuckle. Then again deep into the knuckle of the second finger.

The doctor said: "This will kill the pain!" I wondered as I clenched my teeth tighter, if it was over, but it was not the case. The beautiful blonde nurse turned over my hand to leave the palm facing the white ceiling. It was almost as if I had just lost an Indian arm wrestle on purpose. I'd been exposed! And how!

Reality struck again in the form of two more jabs, this time on either side of the open wound. Now I know what my dog went through — agony!

"Just one more pinprick and it will be finished," said the doctor. Now for the big one —aimed straight into the red flesh itself. I knew this would happen, but hoped he'd forget it!

He wasn't going to do this to me, so I flexed all the muscles in my hand. You little ripper: the needle wouldn't go in. But the pain was still quite excruciating as he withdrew the injection in defeat. He didn't give in though. Moments later, nurse Helen attracted my attention away from the makeshift operating table.

In it went, and it felt like the point of the needle touched the bones in my upper wrist. I had momentarily let down my guard and the 'doc' had succeeded. All that had to be done now was to thread a needle and sew up the gap.

The painkillers were taking effect and all was ready to continue. It was a strange half-moon shaped needle, a bit like a fish hook really, threaded with cat gut I think. Eight times the circle was completed across the torn webbing. Soon the flesh was covered and a cotton dressing applied.

Like most injuries, the cure is worse than the actual injury. So good luck in your sporting future and may your pain be minimal.

23

The Great Cricket Teaser

'WE NEEDED TEN TO WIN, ONE BALL REMAINING IN THE MATCH'

My Dad pulled the well worn cricket ball high and hard.

The Channel Nine cricket statistician, Irving Rosenwater is a man obsessed by the numerical aspects of cricket. His brain is like a computer, spitting out dates, partnerships, wickets and runs with efficiency plus.

His love of the game and his vast knowledge make him the prime target in our commentary box, for what I would call a cricket teaser.

A typical morning prior to the beginning of a Test match will possibly begin with, "Irving, how is it possible to score 'X' off two or three balls?"

Our man hates not knowing the answer, and there have been very few times he's been stumped or caught out by his friends. He even comes up with a few good ones himself! I asked him to try this one for a starter!

How can each opening batsmen on the same team be six not out and the total 0/12 after just two balls of the morning have been bowled by the opening bowler? Remember, there have been no wides or no-balls bowled! No tricks or no scoring mistakes either.

Easy? Not really! The answer is this: The batsman taking strike, hits the ball to deep mid-on for three. The return throw is taken by the bat pad fieldsman standing almost in the centre of the wicket. The umpire signals one-short as they scramble for three and the resulting throw at the bowler's end goes for four overthrows! So after one ball, batsmen No. 1 is six not out and now at the striker's end after running three.

Off the second ball of the day, batsman No. 2 hooks the bouncer for six, and the scoreboard states clearly both batsmen are six not out and the total 0/12. How about that!

I stumped Irving with this one too — "How could my Dad score 10 runs off just one ball?"

First of all he asked if it was a first-class match. I said, "Not bloody likely, 20 years ago in Tasmania!"

Then the wheels in his head started to turn, his eyes focused on the ceiling . . . searching . . . "What if they ran three, got another three off overthrows, and then a further four further overthrows?"

That's fair enough but when I canned the idea of no balls, wides and overthrows, he went an ashen-grey colour around the eyes.

You see, what happened was this . . . my Dad pulled the well-worn leather cricket ball high and hard through mid-wicket. We needed 10 to win, one ball remaining in the match. True!

Much to my old man's surprise, the small cork, inner core of the cricket ball, with string intact, went flying over the crude boundary line and into the coarse prickle bushes on the full. Six runs!

Now, wait for it — the loose leather jacket, looking like a fluffy half-opened scallop shell, just had enough momentum and pace to trickle into the fence for four!

Add the two scores together, because they both occurred simultaneously off the same delivery and you've got 10 runs. As I often said it could only happen in Tasmania!

Having then whet Irving's appetite for the unusual, I couldn't help but tell him of another occasion where Big Max, my father, steered us home to victory with a 10 off the second last ball.

This was in a semi-final game of Sunday afternoon competition — hardly Benson and Hedges World Series Cup stuff, but it was certainly a good, clean, healthy and very competitive level of cricket.

The biggest problem in most of these games used to be clearing up the cow-pats from the area close to our home-made concrete wicket. There's nothing worse than diving to your right or left in the covers, and ending up with your nose in a fresh, warm, soggy pile of cow dung.

Nevertheless, the cows are very handy because most of our paddocks didn't justify the expense of a curator — so it had to be either cows or goats, and they did the trick! The only problem with goats is that they love the taste of willow cricket bats and leather cricket balls . . . it was goodnight if any gear happened to be left lying around!

My old man was captain of a social team selected from patrons of the Empire Hotel — he was the proprietor and of course supplied all of the liquid refreshments.

As you may well imagine most of the best cricket in these games is played late in the day when all the Dutch courage and confidence emerges. And not always with success.

That Sunday's proceedings went along very well, especially the morning session, and everyone had fun and a drink.

When someone tallied up the score card (that was on the back of a piece of cardboard) we became aware of an intriguing situation. The Empire Hotel needed 10 runs to win, and importantly there were two balls remaining.

I could sense the atmosphere around the ground. Everyone momentarily put down their amber-filled glasses waiting in anticipation, kids stopped playing and the dogs began howling. Electric!

The opposition bowler charged in to bowl off an unusually long run, his pocket full of car keys sounding like an eccentric belting away on a xylophone. I can still see the frenzied look on his purple face after running so far just to deliver one ball — a sort of distorted agony and ecstasy!

Big Max was on strike and I was down at the bowler's end, backing up on nought not out! My old man immediately got on the front foot . . . his size 12 sandshoes not quite to the pitch of the ball, but his eyes were focused clearly on the well-worn cherry. It was so worn out that it looked more like a rag doll than a cricket ball.

The attempted cover drive wasn't exactly out of the 'Art of Cricket', by Sir Donald Bradman. Dad's flashing blade could only manage a thick inside edge and the ball gently trickled away behind the square leg umpire, towards the fence.

We both took off and ran like hell, turned for two, looked for three, even four. When it came to the sixth run, I said to my partner, "That's it dad, we can only run six!"

"Bullshit son," he replied, "just keep on running!" And so we did!

While we were scampering for runs, four or five fieldsman had gathered in the long grass down by the fine leg fence. We just kept on running. By the time we'd run all 10 necessary to win the game, about eight guys were stooped in a circle about 60 metres off the bat, at long leg.

My dad was suffering from heartburn and dyspepsia — it's not every day a batsman gets to run 10 in a row. We'd won the match with a ball to spare! "You little beauty!" I loved to win in those days, and I still do today!

Before we left the pitch, curiosity got the better of us . . . there were now 10 players standing in a tight circle at deep fine leg up to their ankles in grass.

Yes! There it was. The lonely old cricket ball dead smack in the middle of a curled up tiger snake.

There was no way known that any of those blokes was going to put his hand down to pick up the ball!

Irving looked at me strangely. Maybe I am a touch warped, but my goodness, I did have a lot of fun playing cricket in the early days.

The Importance of Nudes

'IT WAS A LOT EASIER SKETCHING FAT GIRLS THAN SKINNY MEN'

My Dad was a master builder in Hobart during my formative years, before the hotel days, and I guess he was singularly responsible for pointing me in the right direction of architecture as a career when he professed to me: "Son, there's not much money in the building game — you'd be far better off being an architect."

I had already spent many days tagging along in the shadow of my Dad's builder's overalls and at 12 years of age I could tell the difference between a floor joist, a rafter and a stump.

My appetite for knowledge continued at a healthy rate and soon I was the proud owner of a magnificent custom-made, cedar drawing board complete with T-square and pencil holder.

The first big design to flow from that creative platform was simply titled 'Maxie's Motel' — a 14 bedroom affair which aesthetically did not make the heart beat faster.

Architecture is a fascinating course of study — it covers such a wide range of subjects. It consists of not just the basic art and building subjects, but also important areas like sociology, psychology, law, accountancy and communication — 46 subjects in all, over a six-year period of qualification.

It was during this time that my life was coloured and enriched by some incredible characters. What made it all the more exciting was the fact that I had crossed Bass Strait to live on the mainland.

My first day at the Royal Melbourne Institute of Technology was memorable, considering I had been educated at the very formal Friends' School in Hobart where the teachers all wore flowing black robes and the Quaker background meant they were very strict in the classroom.

By comparison the lecture room at RMIT was different. I turned up on the first day wearing a houndstooth sports jacket and tie . . . the rest wore blue jeans and a variety of billboard style T-shirts! It didn't take long to learn.

Nevertheless I couldn't come to grips with smoking, eating pies and drinking cans of Coca Cola during a lesson. Nor could I relate to the rowdy group playing cards at the back of the class.

Still as one of the lecturers said that day, "I get paid whether you listen or not!" It was pretty good advice to the 73 ambitious adolescents with plans of becoming future architects.

By year three, or the half way mark, 40 of them had been culled from the list of hopefuls and only seven realised their goals of qualifying on time.

Year three was the year nude sketching classes appeared on the timetable for the first time.

The philosophy being that if you can draw the human body naked and in correct proportion, then you will be able to draw anything! Having

27

attempted to sketch a variety of shapes from either sex I must say it's not easy!

I'll never forget our first session with live models. Here we were in the middle of a Melbourne winter poised with our cream-coloured butcher's paper clipped on to our masonite, artist support boards, clutching a handful of sharpened pencils and gathered around an empty classroom stage.

Then she appeared — black silk dressing gown, bright red hair, blue eyes, a little nervous and definitely a lover of fast foods — at least two stone over weight! Nevertheless off came the gear. She had heavily freckled fair skin.

We were given only seven minutes to complete our first pencil sketch of the young woman now sitting on a stool reading a novel in front of a single bar strip radiator.

The majority of the class sat bolt upright, with eyeballs straining for a better look and mouths gaping wide . . . apart from our three female classmates who couldn't hold back their embarrassed giggles.

Five minutes had elapsed and I didn't know where to draw the first line . . . begin at her feet or give the young lady a face first?

Yes, that initial attempt was terrible considering I spent five minutes staring at the woman and only two minutes drawing.

Next was a scrawny looking male model — all ribs and a large hook nose!

The girls amongst us giggled louder as the rest of us struggled with our 6B pencils. Somehow my impressions of this bloke didn't look anything like they were supposed to . . .

Gee, I was glad we didn't have to show the models our work. As these very popular classes continued, we were often told a good gauge of the artist's ability is whether or not he'd show the finished sketch, sign it and hang it in a public place. Well, it took a long time to feel that comfortable about my work and I must confess it was a lot easier sketching fat girls than skinny men.

Early in the course, as part of the creative process, we were asked to build several abstract models — we had to interpret into a three-dimensional coloured model, the senses of smell, sight, taste, touch and sound, experienced during a compulsory stroll through the Block Arcade in Melbourne.

I set about my assignment in cardboard with great enthusiasm. And after seven or eight hours' labour I was proud of my efforts.

The time soon arrived for all of us to display our masterpieces under the watchful eye of a man I shall call Bernie — a pear-shaped lecturer with a penchant for cigars and red wine. His favorite outfit was always capped off with a black, leather waistcoat and rather loose fitting trousers which were continually yanked from behind by their owner at short irritating intervals. Most people have nervous twitches, Bernie just had loose trousers.

He took one look at my model, one thump with a clenched fist, and the colourful cardboard arcade look-alike was demolished right before my watery eyes.

"If I wanted a scale model of the Block Arcade I'd have asked for a scale model of the Block Arcade —clear?" he shouted.

"Start again and think about it this time!" he bellowed.

My face went crimson with embarrassment, but I learned to think about exactly what he said in future. In my opinion, Bernie not only was one of the real characters lecturing in architecture at RMIT, but one of our best design tutors.

He was constantly looking for originality in work and hated copying. So did we as students for that matter but all of us need stimulation to spark the idea of creativity.

One day all hell broke loose during a fourth year crit of our design assignments. Each one had been carefully pinned up on the wall ready for discussion.

Several went under Bernie's scrutiny prior to lunch. Then during the break a few of my friends decided one of the submissions was unfair! In fact, it was a direct copy from a recent magazine — even the notes relating to the concept were in a similar position!

So what did the rest of the class do about it? They cut out the page exposing the offending sketch and pinned it directly above the copy. The reaction of the lecturer was predictable —right off the top! Apart from the humiliation of being exposed in front of fellow students, the offender was failed. We all learned quite a lot from that episode.

On the practical side we all had to have a dash at oxy-acetylene and arc welding . . . this isn't as easy as it looks either.

I suppose the highlight of this six-week stint was our first day in the workshop. Everyone turned up wondering what was going to happen —our three female students as well —dressed neatly in their sheer mesh nylon stockings.

Well, after an hour of arc welding, sparks flying everywhere, they left the lesson with legs looking like Dalmation dogs — big black spots where the sparks had landed on the nylons. The following week, like the lads — it was a case of wearing jeans all round!

After qualifying in 1973, I tackled the world of cricket and took the opportunity to see how different countries solved their architectural problems —and there certainly was a fair variety —from the sound bamboo buildings of the West Indies to the primitive thatched roof dwellings in South Africa. I had a chance to compare American skyscrapers with the Gothic cathedrals of Europe.

Yes, I really did take time out from my cricket tours to talk to architects and to look at their work. Mind you, I didn't once get accompanied by Dougie Walters, Rodney Marsh or Dennis Lillee — they preferred to relax in a different manner, usually poolside with a beer.

Running into a Fan

'THERE WERE ONLY TWO WHEELS ANYWHERE NEAR THE GROUND'

Like most young adolescents I couldn't wait until the day I turned 18 — old enough to legally drive a car. Looking back on a career spanning almost 20 years behind the steering wheel of a great variety of vehicles I can honestly say that motor cars are both expensive and dangerous.

I'm still alive, to describe some of my close encounters of the four wheel kind, but not without a fair amount of luck.

The first new car I owned in Melbourne was a beautiful box-like, but shining white VE Valiant, or as the boys would call it — the Greek Mercedes. It really should have been a VD Valiant, because the previous year's model was given the initials VC. Maybe the sexual overtones were too hot to handle for the manufacturer, Chrysler.

Anyway what's in a name — I loved this pure white machine with all my heart. I had qualified for my driver's licence in amongst the hardly bustling 4.30 p.m. peak hour traffic of Hobart, 18 months earlier. So, by comparison, the congestion and driver aggression of downtown Melbourne was a frightening experience for a young fella from Tasmania.

Add to that the peculiar right hand turns that could only be made from a left hand lane and the overall result was one of fearful confusion . . . so much so that I only had the confidence to drive my brand new showpiece once or twice around the block in Camberwell, where I lived.

Then when I did eventually, take it into town, for the first bit trip, it happened — smash! A bingle. Yes, in the back streets of Collingwood, a stupid driver in a blue Falcon, failed to give way to his right. Even though I stood firmly on my brake pedal, the sparkling body work and chrome grille came to rest crumpled and hard up against the other driver's front door and fender.

Words failed me at the time, especially when he hopped confidently out of his undamaged passenger side door, and confronted me with the unexpected words, "You're Maxie Walker aren't you? I barrack for Melbourne . . . gee I'm sorry."

My radiator had obviously burst. Everywhere on the road was broken glass and tell-tale leaking water. Within seconds a tow truck operator appeared from nowhere and wanted my signature on his pink pad! It was all happening a bit quick for me . . . I still couldn't believe my pride and joy was buried in the rib-cage of this other person's rust-bucket!

The crunch came when I had to ask my Dad for the taxi-fare home! He wasn't a happy father. After all, he was the one who told me to be careful if I drove past the corner at the end of our street.

It's not a good idea to drive when you're tired either. Again, I learned the hard way.

After entertaining a large gathering of middle management executives at a Marysville Guest House some two hours from Melbourne, in the middle of winter, I set off into the fog for the warmth and comfort of my own bed.

Visibility must have been limited to no more than 10 metres. I followed the snaking white line as best I could considering the circumstances.

Somewhere along the way, I must have taken a wrong turn, because the big Ford I was driving was sliding around hairpin bends on the muddy surface of a narrow graded road which was beginning to wind its way down the mountainside.

Inside my car the heater was blowing hot air around my feet and the windows were beginning to fog up. I felt warm and comfortable. Then, I must have closed my weary eyes for a brief moment because I woke up with a start only to feel the car sliding off the road into a deep culvert.

It unfortunately came to rest at about 45 degrees to the shoulder of the road, and at the same time my body lunged forward and thudded into the steering wheel. The impact left very little wind in my lungs — the same sort of feeling as being hit head-on, or shirt-fronted on the football field.

There were only two wheels anywhere near the ground and they were firmly entrenched in the ditch on the passenger's side. The other two were motionless, and muddied, about a metre off the surface of the road.

Gee, what was a bloke going to do now, a million miles from anywhere at

31

1 a.m. in the morning? Anyway there I was, stranded in the bush for all the animals and birds to laugh at.

Most important though was the fact that I wasn't badly hurt. Sure my car looked out of business but I shudder to think how it might have ended had the car left the road on the right hand side where there was a very steep fall — all I could see through the mist was a wall of gum tree tops.

Isn't it strange? When I needed a tow truck they were nowhere to be seen! I thought of the RACV but the biggest problem was the distinct lack of public telephones on this frontier road.

I've heard of people being able to lift cars with feats of super-human strength when in trouble . . . well, I was definitely in trouble but do you reckon I could summon that superhuman strength?

Common sense prevailed and at approximately 3 a.m., after a couple of hours shivering in the cold night air, I decided it was time to stop hoping a car might come by, so it was back into the car to try and sleep.

Sleep didn't come easily. Obviously my wife would be worried to death at my absence — I was expected home at about 2 o'clock.

Morning arrived all too slowly with a beautiful chorus of bird calls and ice on the windows —what a start to the day!

When I finally did hear the beautiful sound of an engine it was after 8 a.m. I anxiously peered at the pea soup fog waiting for help to appear . . . you little beauty!

It was a farmer and his wife in an old Bedford utility truck. They could have been Dave and Mabel. They stopped as soon as they realised I belonged to the badly parked car and were eager to help. Thank goodness they didn't recognise me!

The rural couple were just fantastic — they hooked up my front bumper bar to their tow-bar, with a rusty old chain. Quick as a flash, my car was back on the muddy road . . . and even though it was extensively damaged on the passenger side, it was still driveable.

The damaged front wheel was a bit wobbly but provided I kept the speeds below 30 kmh there was a good chance I would be able to limp home. And that's exactly what I did, ever so slowly.

By the time I reached the Maroondah Highway in Lilydale, the peak hour traffic was still pretty heavy. Cars were banked up behind for kilometres. Horns were honking and talk about glares. I wished, for the time being that I was a jockey, barely able to see out of the windows.

And talking about jockeys, one of my friends was a jockey. A little fella named Peter Bakos. He's only about four foot nothing and if he picks me up to drive to a speaking engagement, he just walks across the bench seat and opens the passenger door for me! The brake and accelerator pedals are specially built up with blocks of wood so he can reach them!

Then when it's my turn to provide the transport I always leave the kids' bucket seat in the back so he can see out of the windows . . . he loves me doing the driving.

Anyway enough about jockeys. I did manage to guide my car home only to be greeted with a barrage of expected questions. You can probably guess the first one! "And where have you been all night?" asked my wife with a not too friendly tone in her voice.

It took a lot of explaining.

So these days I'm much more careful about driving long distances. And fatigue — it's easy to see why it's a killer.

Chapter Two

SOMETIMES THE JOKES WERE ON ME

Richie's younger brother had an unusually colourful command of the English language.

Some Bellyaches on Tour
'ALL THIS LIVESTOCK TENDED TO MAKE CONDITIONS A LITTLE CROWDED'

Money can't buy an overseas trip with the Australian cricket team. Every young cricketer in Australia I bet has at some stage dreamt of touring England with the Test team.

Well in my case it was a tour of the Caribbean that came first — in 1973. It was the first time a touring side ventured abroad without at least one veteran player who had visited that particular country at some stage during his career.

I will never forget that trip for many reasons.

One of them was Johnny Watkins who, at the age of 29 was also making his first (and only) tour. His selection came in for a great deal of criticism both before and after the team left for the West Indies.

Poor old 'Wok'. He only played in seven games for the tour and didn't get a guernsey for any of the Tests: but he did achieve a certain degree of success in the games he did play and finished up with 17 wickets at 27.23.

Johnny also featured rather prominently in a couple of 'incidents' during the tour which centred around two or three of the more incorrigible practical jokers in the party. Blokes like the poker-faced Doug Walters who Johnny Watkins idolised. Nevertheless Dougie was the greatest practical joker of them all.

At the completion of Wok's first over in Test cricket, just weeks before against Pakistan in the 3rd Test at the Sydney Cricket Ground — Dougie struck out with his usual wit.

The over was a maiden but included three wides from the Newcastle leg-spinner and, as he walked past his mate Dougie Walters at mid-off, pulling his jumper over his head, Doug said, "Thanks for trying out the wicket for the Shield match next door Wok!! It looks as though it's taking a bit of spin eh?"

The very much tongue-in-cheek comment was typical of Walters . . .

Our first game on West Indian soil was quite a notable event. It was a one day match against the University of the West Indies to be played at the Mona campus oval. Though to be calling it an oval would be paying it an unfair compliment. It was more like a country claypan.

During the course of any match in Australia you can expect to be held up on the odd occasion when a small dog finds its way on to the ground — but Mona campus! It was only a small ground by any standards; but in addition to the 13 cricketers and two umpires, there were three cows, half a dozen goats, a few chooks and a dense flock of very large birds overhead that Stackie (Keith Stackpole) declared were buzzards. All this livestock tended to make conditions a little cramped.

Notwithstanding the unfavourable cricket environment, it was an

35

encouraging start, considering that we were all still pretty stiff from the long flight from Australia.

I know I creaked like an unoiled door as I threw the arm over for my first delivery. It was slow, straight, and deserved to be hit for six. Sebastian was the bloke's name and he leant back and cut the ball straight into first slip where Ian Chappell completed the catch. So I can say that I took a wicket with my very first ball in the West Indies.

In the meantime Bob Massie, who would without a doubt have been the fussiest eater amongst the lot of us, had somehow contrived to pick up some sort of stomach complaint and had been carted off to hospital for a few days.

From the tales that Redders (Ian Redpath) had told us about the food in India during his tour there, we were fairly well off by comparison: though we had been warned not to sample anything from the numerous street stalls, but to confine our eating to the motel. So we were all mystified about Bob's illness.

After he was discharged, the doctor ruled that he would have to spend a few days recuperating by the hotel pool.

By this time we were playing the second game of the tour, against Jamaica at Sabina Park, where we got our first look at local hero, Lawrence Rowe, and a pretty quick youngster named Michael Holding. In later years he was known simply as 'Whispering Death'.

Our transport too and from the ground was an ancient, dilapidated red bus. It had no windows and more rattles than a millionaire's baby; but a real fun machine and great for singing our own versions of the popular songs of the day. One of our favorites, which ultimately became our theme song for the tour, was 'My Ding-a-ling.'

We had managed to do a little reciprocal deal with the local brewers, and keg of the local brew, Red Stripe, had been installed outside the room occupied by Doug Walters and Terry Jenner.

When we'd arrive back at the end of the day's play, in full chorus, we'd invariably find Bob sitting by the pool with a glass in his hand, feet up and with half a dozen waiters hovering about, obviously enjoying his 'recuperation' to the full.

Actually that barrel was a little too conveniently situated. A few of the waiters got into the habit of inviting a bunch of their friends around during the day in the happy belief that we required some assistance to lower the level. This had unfortunate results when they merrily attempted to juggle tray, jug and glasses.

After about three days of hard toil and arriving back at the hotel to see Bob 'recuperating', his room-mate John Benaud challenged him about his recovery rate.

Bob's reply was along the lines of still having terrible gastric and diahorrea troubles . . . "haven't been off the dunny seat all day mate!"

Now you can imagine what John Benaud said, when he discovered the house-maid's paper seal still intact on the toilet seat in their en-suite ... well, maybe you can't because Richie's younger brother had an unusually colourful command of the English language with adjectives being his big 'go'! I think he got out five different ones all in the same sentence.

Next morning Bob Massie was on the bus with the rest of us and the Red Stripe barrel untouched.

First Minutes in the Green and Gold

'THE MAJORITY OF THESE CHARACTERS WOULD BECOME MY GREAT MATES'

The enthusiastic queues of bright-eyed spectators waited patiently to gain entry into the MCG for the gladiatorial contest between Australia and Pakistan in January, 1973.

I tried to look cool, calm and collected as I made my way to the player's entrance but it wasn't easy! Today I would play my first Test match, and my heart was predictably pounding nervously inside my ribcage.

The MCC official operating the old-fashioned green turnstile wished me good luck ... I was only a 100 or so steps away from the Australian dressing room door, and I wondered what sort of reaction I would get from the other players when I entered the room? Arnie Beitzel, the room attendant, opened the door marked 'Australian Dressing Room' — I thought this is it! It was the realisation of a life-long dream. But what should I do now?

There was no fuss, everyone just went on doing their own thing ... and Arnie had left me standing alone in the middle of the room.

If only I could have known at that moment that during the next decade the majority of these characters would become my great mates and form the nucleus of a very successful Australian team.

My first mistake was to claim a locker that had been the property of Doug Walters for quite a few Tests. It's funny how superstition and an unwillingness to change almost preoccupies sportsmen in their locker rooms! Well, cricketers are even worse because they spend so much time in the dressing room — especially if they don't bat very well.

Anyway, by the time I had handed in my valuables and then grabbed a cup of tea like a few other lads, Dougie Walters arrived.

Doug had nicely settled into his locker as if it was his divine right and my shirt and jumper were not so politely dumped on the cotton weave carpet floor. Next question, where was my kitbag and my gear? There were many suggestions, one of which stated bluntly — the WC.

Sure enough, my beautiful, brand new green and gold vinyl bag was sticking out of the shining white bowl. Because of its size the end didn't touch the water line but just the same it was a bit of a shock.

Any nerves I might have had were quickly forgotten amongst the cheers and laughing that erupted behind.

This was my first taste of full-blooded green and gold Aussie team spirit that bonded us together under Ian Chappell's influence.

The eyelines of my new team-mates were now all locked into mine, searching for a reaction — had they pressed the wrong button, how was I coping or was I just very upset about the whole damn incident? The answer no! My developing years as a VFL footballer with the Melbourne Football Club had conditioned me to expect anything from team-mates in a change room.

Now it was up to me to win their respect. The best way to do that was certainly to take a few wickets and score a few runs.

But here in the dressingroom, there are many unwritten rules, I had just broken one — don't pinch a senior player's locker!

In many ways the hierarchy system which exists between cricketers in a Test match is similar to that in the animal world where the lion is king of the beasts.

The main man in our structure definitely was Ian Chappell. Next were the more experienced players, then the new boys like myself and the 12th man — he had to do everything he was told. Expected to be the first at the ground and last to leave without batting or bowling in the match.

The other thing frowned upon by most captains is where you scribble a signature on a sheet of paper, bat or autograph book.

I made the 'blue' of signing at the top of the bats and books pretty early on in my career. It may have been Ian Chappell who sarcastically stated, "How bloody long have you been captain of Australia, Tangles?" The message gets home very quickly.

The hierarchy works even better on tour, in places like London, where there is the opportunity to go along to other great sporting events like the FA Cup final at Wembley or Wimbledon.

No prizes for guessing who picks up the three free passes to sit centre court and witness the men's or women's final either — captain, vice-captain and third selector. They have the power to organise which games they want off and nine times out of 10 their three days off coincide with one or more of these finals or a day at Ascot having a bet.

The senior pro's always get to sit in the front row for team photgraphs, although Dougie Walters used to cause more trouble that it was worth. The boy from Dungog used to be a constant problem for photographers. If he didn't place an extra cricket boot between his own two feet he'd have a packet of Rothman's cigarettes subtly protruding from his shirt pocket. Leave him in the back row and the practical joker would be even worse.

One day at the MCG Dougie discreetly placed several plastic dog's droppings on the shoulders of two front row players! Needless to say they weren't noticed until the photographs were printed and mounted on official card at quite some cost. Just as the third boot and cigarettes had done in the past.

I also quickly found out that when a batsman like Keith Stackpole is given out LBW just short of a century and he swats a chair in the dressing room with his bat so hard that all four legs are missing — you don't laugh, in fact one doesn't even smile.

I learnt to never speak to Ian Chappell within 30 minutes of him getting out, particularly if it was a bad shot. Several press men found out the hard way.

Also it was not a good idea to comment on the aesthetic qualities of the women sitting in front of the players area. Many a good batsman has come undone talking about a new player's wife, sister, girlfriend or mum.

So there you are — there's a lot to think about even before a 'first gamer' walks onto the sacred turf to represent Australia.

Not Out on the News Desk
'IN A WAY, I WAS THE HOPE OF THE SIDE'

Reading sports news for the first time on television for GTV-9 in Melbourne would have to be one of the most nerve-wracking experiences I've had in a long time.

There I was, seated behind the news desk at the studios with barely a minute remaining in the commercial break.

Finally, the floor manager counted me down with his extended fingers just below the intimidating lens of Camera No. 3. "Five, four, three, two, one ...!" The red light on top of the camera lit up like an ambulance — it's now or never!

Seated next to me was the doyen of newsreaders in Victoria, 'Brian told me' Naylor. He was immaculately dressed as always with not a hair out of place and it appeared not a nerve in his body.

Brian had completed his world and local read in a very professional manner, then with a brief introduction to my newsreading career he said, "and now for sport here's Max Walker!"

It is very difficult to put into words just how I felt at that moment. My right hand had hold of my left in a vice-like grip for comfort, displaying eight white knuckles to the camera. The lump in my throat was now up around my ears — in fact I thought for a moment I may have had mumps!

Yes, I was certainly nervous ... it began earlier in the day as I discussed what topics were newsworthy with John Sorell the news director and my immediate boss Rob Syme, a man of extensive journalistic experience.

By the time Terry, Brian Naylor's make-up man, began to apply the 'Boy George' look-alike stuff to my face, about 30 minutes before the news began, the butterflies in my stomach had reached plague proportions!

The ones I had deep in my belly must have been the ones with large wings.

I'm told it's not a bad feeling before a performance to get butterflies in your stomach — except the trick is to get them in a group formation and flying in a straight line. Well I can honestly say the variety of butterflies I had deep in my belly, must have been ones with large wings, because it felt like they were knocking the daylight out of my stomach lining.

As I actually spoke, I wanted to say, "G'day," but opted to do the right thing and say, "Good evening!"

At that very moment, my life and everything that I had been told to do flashed before my eyes at an extraordinary pace — here I was the end product of much behind the scenes expertise. In a way I was the hope of the side! A bit like being a nightwatchman for Australia in a crucial Test match.

All that is needed is to occupy the crease for seven or eight minutes up until stumps . . . that's about the duration I had to sit behind the desk and read the sporting news.

Anyone who's ever attempted either would realise that neither is an easy task. The eyes of all and sundry are focused on the determination of the person to succeed — and not make a mistake. I think they call it perfection and it's very difficult to achieve!!!

Taking block in the middle of the MCG with just the bat in your hands — eight minutes to go and a crazy fast bowler charging towards the wicket —takes a lot of courage. In fact, the more I thought about my stint behind the television camera as a newsreader, the more parallels I kept coming up with — all related to the nightwatchman theory.

Anyhow, It was pleasing to read for the first time on my home ground, Melbourne. And I must say what a great feeling it was to be accepted into the team at GTV-9 so readily.

When Australia was arguably the best cricket team in the world in the mid-70's, our biggest single strength, was our team spirit. There definitely was a similar spirit in the newsroom.

All that aside, I had to continue to tell the sports stories as I saw them and to introduce the videotape pictures describing each event in the news.

At one stage I felt my eyes must have looked like a dead fish's — the glare of the lights and the huge television camera lens looking straight up my nostrils wasn't too comfortable. I could feel myself rushing a bit . . . firstly the cricket story, was easy. Then the football . . . I got my tongue stuck around one word . . . I can't remember which and I thought, don't blow it now Maxie! Yes, I proved I was human, but you're not supposed to stumble — but with a nickname like Tanglefoot I guess it was going to happen sooner or later. Better sooner.

I tried to relax as I approached the daily double, Bert Bryant's tips and finally the quadrella. I reckon I'm going to have some fun pronouncing some of the more flamboyant horse names as they win, I thought.

I did remain not-out at stumps that night thanks to everyone in the team. It meant a lot to me.

Footnotes to a Sporting Life

'*I FAINTED AND FELL FACE FIRST TOWARDS THE FLOOR*'

For anyone who has attempted success and fame through sport, the common denominator would have to be pain. It would be fair to say pain is a constant companion to the committed sportsperson.

The greatest fast bowler the game of cricket has ever produced, Dennis Lillee, once said: "If you're fit enough to walk through the gates, then you're fit enough to play!"

But, what if you can't stand up, can't walk or just plain can't make it?

Every time I received an injury whether it was a knee, back, neck or arm injury, I reckoned at the time that the ailing limb or joint was the most important part of my body. This was possibly because all the pain had localised and my thoughts were dominated by this one negative aspect of my body.

How then did I used to treat little things like blisters and in-grown toenails? If I answer honestly, I would have to say gingerly.

I often managed to end up with an ingrown toenail or two. I think the first time I grew one was a direct result of my biting my toenails. Can you imagine that? Or can you imagine me with my big toe in my mouth? Don't try! In those days I was just a very supple kid.

Imagine if I'd studied and even practised yoga! Maybe my action might have been a bit smoother, instead of bowling right arm over left earhole, with my legs crossed in the delivery stride? Still, it's pretty difficult to be good looking and pretty on your feet as well!

I matured very slowly and by the ripe old age of 19, when I was just learning to shave (although I didn't need to), I was taking my sport very seriously, especially my football!

Perhaps I was guilty of neglecting my feet at the expense of the 'fluff' on my face. The result was an in-grown toenail. Just what I didn't need at the beginning of the 1967 football season with so much fitness work and kicking of the football to do.

Yes, it did hurt to kick! It hurt a lot. It even hurt just to put my street shoes on . . . thongs were more the order of the day!

So I fronted up to practice one cold and wet Tuesday night in April '67 hoping not to have to train. I walked into the medical room only metres past the numbered, grey metal lockers in the Melbourne Football Club's dressing room at the MCG.

The first bloke I ran into was our medico, Bob Ashbey, who took one look and referred me to our physiotherapist at the time. We used to go through them like half-back flankers!

After asking the educated man if it was possible to give me a couple of pills to fix up my badly festered toe, he said, "The medical profession has come a long way but unfortunately for you — not that far!"

He confirmed my worst thoughts — there was no pill in the world capable of fixing an inflamed and badly infected in-grown toenail!

Which made me reflect on how it happened . . . I really don't know! I'm sure I cut the little 'v' in the middle of the nail. Maybe I hadn't cut the toe-nail square with the end of that ugly hammer-head toe on my right foot. Yes, I did everything a young footballer ought to do. All these thoughts weren't going to fix my toe though.

Confront the problem like a man, I kept telling myself, unfortunately the club doctor didn't appear at training that evening. This meant I had all night to think about what the Doc might have to do to fix it. A warped imagination didn't help either.

My confrontation with Dr Colin Galbraith, the footy club doctor, turned out to be pretty horrific. After exchanging the normal pleasantries in the consulting rooms at the rear of his house, we got down to business.

There I was sitting on a very low stool, exposing my foot for him to inspect. Expecting the worst, I was naturally on edge. And when he grabbed my big toe in his right hand it was like levitation — I rose about 18 inches off the stool in response to the acute pain!

They tell me doctors sometimes have to be cruel to be kind — they're not wrong. When he put me down, the doctor said in a jovial manner: "I've got just the thing to fix this up my boy!"

He walked away to the antique, roll-top desk that all doctors seem to have. All I could hear and see was what appeared to be a rearranging of papers. When he finally turned around, there before my eyes was . . . this huge needle about six inches long!

Before I could prevent my cold-hearted friend from grabbing my toe, he had a vice-like grip on it. Then with a great deal of conviction, almost pleasure, the silver haired, bespectacled doctor plunged the shiny silver needle deep into the heart of my now throbbing toe — the pain was excruciating to say the least and this was supposed to be a pain-killing injection. I wanted to shout, but no sound came forth.

And then he opted for a second slice of the action. This time he pushed the pain killer into the top of the rather red big toe. At this stage, not only was a yellow looking liquid seeping from the edge of the toe-nail, but my eyes were beginning to well with moisture.

I almost passed out when the third and final jab scored a direct hit from below the toe.

It seemed like eternity before the pain deadened. Now for the real heavy stuff! The doctor began to cut out the offending piece of jagged nail from deep in the edge of my numb toe. I was still conscious . . . surgical scissors doing their job — a precise cut was made parallel to the edge of my toe. Then a change of tactics — the right angled scissors were produced. Blood was freely flowing from the wound now and I didn't like it!

The good doctor continued with a right angled cut — at this stage it was too much! I fainted and fell face first towards the floor.

Quickly I was helped to a nearby couch, before I came to, feeling very groggy . . . I know it's only an in-grown toe-nail but the pain was unbearable. 'Never again!' I said to myself as I left the surgery.

Quite incredibly the same nail and toe became infected again . . . and we did it all over again a week or two later — and it wasn't any easier the second time around.

That kept me out of action for three weeks — we don't appreciate how important our feet are! Do we?

Grass Growing, Seagulls Landing

'WHEN I FINALLY SANK INTO MY POSITION MY NERVES WERE SHOT'

Alan McGilvray: *the voice*

How does a first class cricketer, especially one qualified in the profession of architecture, become a member of the poison typewriter club? That is the name most cricketers generally use in reference to the printed media — and some commentators. Use the right tone of voice, and commentary can be quite cunning and caustic!

Yet today, several summers away from the first class arena, I find myself a fully-fledged member of the poison typewriter club as a cricket commentator.

The direction of my life has been drawn like a magnet towards the media.

Unfortunately this has meant a departure from my profession of architect. Maybe the demand for architect-designed chook houses with a 30-degree, sloping metal deck roof is not so great today!

After my retirement as a player I made my debut as a cricket commentator at Kardinia Park, Geelong, in January, 1982. Drew Morphett and I covered the match between Victoria and South Australia for ABC-TV from 10.59 am on Day 1 till 6 pm at the end of Day 4!

It really was a gruelling initiation. The wicket at Geelong was perfect, hundreds of runs were scored between many slow moments. I can tell you that it was difficult describing grass growing, seagulls landing, and the odd stray dog trespassing onto the field at fine leg.

At the end of the game Drew, my senior commentator, was asked how the 'big fella' had performed? "This bloke's unreal," Drew replied. "He can talk underwater with a mouthful of marbles!"

Several weeks later I found myself progressing to a one-day international between Australia and the West Indies in front of a huge crowd at the MCG.

On that occasion I shared the commentary box with the doyen of Australian commentators, Alan McGilvray. I'm sure I was more nervous of fronting up in the commentary box than I was before my first Test match almost a decade before on this very same ground.

Just before going on air, 'Mac' gave me some invaluable advice. "Son," he said, "if you imagine you are talking to a blind man when describing the game you will do alright — call it colour radio."

I have used Mac's words in combination with my own philosophy that it is invariably easier to be an armchair critic than actually be out in the middle doing all the hard work.

Now, before each day's play commences, I write at the top of my notepaper next to the microphone: *"Cricket played at this level is a very difficult game!!!"*

Those words I hope help me to get the contest into the right perspective.

I have been lucky enough to listen to and meet three of cricket's greatest commentators in Alan McGilvray, England's John Arlott and South African Charles Fortune. All three of these gentlemen have the ability to improvise and remain unflustered no matter what.

But there are occasionally problems and I've had my share even in such a short career in broadcasting.

During my first one-day international, the ABC commentary box was a very small hothouse, positioned above the sight screen at the top level of the cigar smokers' stand (for MCC members).

As an architect, I offered them free of charge, to re-design what was effectively a 6-foot by 8-foot, split level chook house without the wire mesh! The temperature on that unforgettable day was a boiling 45 degrees Celsius!

In order to occupy my position at the mike I had to climb bodily over the shoulders of both Mac and that ever-reliable master of statistics, Jack Cameron. With a nickname like 'Tanglefoot' it was pretty obvious I was not going to achieve my aim without incident, especially in such a confined space.

My front leg clipped Mac on the back of his head sending his glasses and binoculars flying; the second leg up-ended Jack Cameron's little bag of goodies, which included organised career statistics, binoculars and reference books.

When I finally sank into my position my nerves were shot — I just knew I had upset the other two blokes.

As always they were very sympathetic and helped me through the initial session of play which lasted an hour. When it was time for me to get out, similar misfortune occurred and as well, this time every article of my clothing was sweat-soaked.

My new Pierre Cardin suit, especially obtained for the occasion, looked as if I had been swimming in it! Bad luck about the under the armpit odour — even 'Aeroguard' wouldn't have worked in these conditions!

My work in the media has not been without its moments — some funny and some moving.

During the Adelaide Centenary Test, ABC colleague Jim Maxwell arrived into the commentary box with a batch of Mars bars. He offered one to me and then took his place at the mike, ripping the paper from his chocolate bar, apparently all ready to take a big bite.

I acknowledged him by taking a big mouthful. Jim who was just starting his stint, immediately asked a very short, sharp question. I had trouble for the next 35 seconds or so trying to separate my tongue from the roof of my mouth, my upper teeth from my lower teeth and trying to answer the question.

By this time Jim had put his Mars bar down and swayed away from the mike with his hanky over his mouth in uncontrollable laughter.

Often, especially in Sydney for the night cricket, some of the kinder souls make cakes and send them up to the commentary box. As with the Mars bars, the big decision will always remain when and how to take a bite.

And to those with a devious sense of humor like myself, the object of the evening sometimes is to see just which one of the ball-by-ball commentary team can be caught out with a mouthful of cake.

There also have been some very serious and emotional moments.

During the 5th Test between Australia and the West Indies in Sydney in 1985, Alan McGilvray was calling his 219th Test — his last in Australia.

As the match neared the final stages of a memorable Australian victory we'd already seen the emotional departure of the great Clive Lloyd. The big fella lingered long on his walk from the ground as if to soak in the acknowledgment of the 25,000 spectators for his contribution to the game.

At tea, with only two wickets still intact, it was obvious that this would be Mac's last session of commentary on air. It was my very great pleasure to be rostered on with him.

Alan Marks, the executive producer for ABC cricket, had asked Mac if he would be in the box five minutes early to give some special comments.

The real reason was to hear a special taped tribute to Alan from Prime Minister Bob Hawke. This had to be taped because no-one could pre-determine the conclusion of the Test match or Alan's last leg on air.

Mac settled into his chair when he heard his name come over the public address system.

There was a mix-up. The high-tech electronic scoreboard had begun to broadcast the PM's tribute for all to hear — 45 seconds earlier than ABC radio.

Once Mac had recognised the voice he took off his headphones and pulled the sliding glass windows open in order to hear more. Then we had drama as Alan Marks asked Mac to close the windows and trust him. Firstly he refused — and only agreed when he heard that same voice come through his head-set.

What Bob Hawke had to say obviously moved the veteran commentator . . . Alan looked at me and said quietly "What a wonderful compliment."

Then, just as the game was due to get under way for the final session of play, the diamond-vision screen of the huge electric scoreboard came to life in a kaleidoscope of colour with the words 'Thanks Mac, you are the greatest' etched into the 40,000 light globes that constituted the screen.

Simultaneously 25,000 stood to a man with eyes cast high to Alan McGilvray in the commentary box at the rear of the Sir Donald Bradman stand. Hands above their heads they gave the man who belonged to the voice, who so many people had loved and respected for almost 50 years, a thunderous, standing ovation.

Two balls had been bowled in the middle as we both stood before the crowd. Mac lifted his hands just as royalty would. Here was something very special happening.

Above the roar of the crowd he turned away from the mike choked with emotion and repeated softly, "What have I done to deserve this, I'm just a cricket commentator?"

Alan McGilvray isn't just another commentator — for almost half a century, from the 1938 synthetic Test match broadcasts — he was the undisputed voice of cricket in Australia.

He ended his innings with grace just a few minutes later in the second over when he asked Alan Marks, "Is it possible to have another commentator in the commentary booth please, I would now like to leave."

He just stood up, turned and immediately walked away from Test cricket in Australia.

Then, with his chair momentarily vacant, I was left with three options, remembering that the lump, formerly in my throat, was now somewhere up near my ears and the atmosphere in the enclosed booth was very emotional — as thick as pea soup.

Firstly, I could do a ball-by-ball commentary, something I hadn't attempted in the past; secondly I could give my expert opinion on the last 10 or so deliveries bowled, none of which I'd taken much notice of; or finally, I could put in a few well-earned words of praise.

I opted for the latter.

It might have been difficult for the West Indies batsmen trying to cope with the spin of Bob Holland and Murray Bennett but I can honestly say it was also very difficult batting from behind the mike . .

I was pretty pleased to see Dennis Cometti sit down next to me. He was stunned and speechless as well for about 15 seconds — it seemed like eternity, but as we say in the box, the ball was in his court.

Broad Bats for the Microphone
'THEN I THOUGHT, HERE'S MY BIG CHANCE'

The business of talking to people for the benefit of television and radio audiences is not as easy and laid back as it looks — in fact the confrontation between the interviewer and interviewee is quite often punctuated with the "unexpected"!

Maybe that's why I like my occupation so much — it's a bit like being a bowler — sometimes the strategy's to subtly play to the batsmen's strength in order to find a weakness. And despite all the planning in the world, it is just about impossible to pre-determine what a batsman will ultimately do.

Take Geoff Boycott for example, the former great England batsman. His biggest problem in life was whether or not to play a shot in the first hour or the second hour of a Test match . . . hardly charismatic but very effective (151 first class centuries). Trying to interview some sportsman is a bit like bowling to the English opener's broad bat — very difficult to make much impact!

While I was working for Channel 7 on their colourful Sunday show, *World of Sport,* it was my difficult task to have a chat to the assistant manager of the touring Sri Lankan cricket team, Mr W. Silva.

Before we got around to talking, if you could call it that, we used some very graphic footage of Jeff Thomson and Dennis Lillee terrifying the living daylights out of the 1975 World Cup team at the Oval where two of the Sri Lankan batsmen retired hurt.

My first question to the No. 2 administrator on tour, suggesting a big improvement on the team that represented his country at that time, was "Things have changed since 1975, haven't they?"

"Yes!" was his blunt reply.

Always be prepared with another question . . . just in case, "You have now got some pretty good young batsmen in your line-up?"

Again "Yes!" followed by an agonising pregnant pause and a blank look.

Beads of perspiration were forming on his forehead. I suspected he was nervous so I attempted to relax him with an easier question like, "Have you enjoyed the tour so far?"

While he uttered the mono-syllabic "Yes!" once more, his team was struggling for runs at the MCG against Victoria's pace attack.

"Well, what about the immediate future of Sri Lankan cricket?"

Another enlightening response "It looks good!"

Then I thought, here's my big chance . . . go for the kill Maxie. "Why?" I asked.

But the sweaty palmed assistant manager again did me like a dinner. "Good players."

At this stage the floor manager was giving me the wind up signal.

I quickly thanked the man for joining us on the show and Lou Richards sarcastically and humorously congratulated him on his enlightening answers to some difficult in-depth questions, and then sent him packing with the usual champagne, chocolates and orange juice.

Gee, he looked relieved when it was over, but not half as much as I was. I learned a lot during that harrowing 90 seconds on air — never ask questions that can be answered by just 'Yes!'

So, armed with this valuable information I set off on my own to become another Michael Parkinson.

The following summer Rodney Hogg had bowled like a demon

Rodney Hogg: *never liked being interviewed*

against Pakistan in Perth during the First Test. So he was the likely target for an interview during the Second Test at Brisbane.

Now let's be honest about 'Hoggie' — he's never liked being interviewed, even today. But I thought being an ex-player and a mate everything would be fine. Well, I was partly correct.

I waited like any good reporter should for the customary half hour after stumps.

The sun sets very early in Brisbane in November and the ground was soon in darkness, so floodlights were needed for the chat to be video-taped.

Finally Hoggie agreed to come to the microphone . . . not an ounce of sweat in sight. My introduction was imaginative and sprinkled with several appropriate adjectives to describe the fearsome strike bowler . . . it lasted about 25 seconds.

Only to be greeted with the most unlikely response: "Jesus, those lights are bloody bright Tangles, can't you do something about them?"

I never did get my introduction of Rodney Hogg together quite as polished as the first one.

I did manage to get him to smile once on camera which must have been a career first for the stoney-faced 'quick' — he was mean-looking in full-cry.

Then of course there was the world champion super heavyweight weight-lifter from Bulgaria. Gee, he was a strong boy — I thought the bar holding the weights was going to break, he had so many on it.

The big problem with this outstanding athlete was how do we make a four-way interview via an interpreter look good on television? First I had to ask my question to the interpreter who in turn repeated my words in Bulgarian to the man mountain, who then stumbled over a suitable answer in Bulgarian.

I took a long time even to get a "Yes."

And I knew there was no way John Sorell back at GTV9 News would use the interview. Then just as we were leaving, the big fella started to talk to me in broken English . . . and it turned out that he was a cricket fanatic and suggested he'd love to have a hit on the MCG.

Unfortunately time was against the strongman wielding a cricket bat in anger on the sacred turf, but just the thought of it conjures up some fascinating images in the mind, doesn't it — eat your heart out Viv Richards!

In 1986 it was my duty to cover the story of an exhibition game of Australian football to be played in Japan after the Hawthorn-Carlton Grand Final.

Jack Hamilton the then VFL 'supremo' was to present a genuine, made in Australia, football to the Deputy Mayor of Yokohama. The whole exercise turned out to be fun with the Deputy Mayor and is non-English speaking party entering into the spirit of the occasion.

Again an interpreter was needed to explain what each man had to say to the other as they exchanged gifts. The Deputy Mayor could speak a few words of our language and we got him to answer two simple questions in English with the aid of a bi-lingual idiot-sheet!

Well, this guy wearing a Richmond Football Club jumper was a sensation — he made John Wayne look like an amateur when it came to reading lines.

Naturally I answered the questions for him and he merely returned those very same words back to camera . . . after only two takes or attempts.

Even the super confident Mark Jackson of VFL football and media fame has had his difficulties so I'm told, with the interview.

Two years before, 'Jacko', as he is known to his masses of fans, refused to do a live radio interview on the grounds that he was sick and tired of being misquoted by the press . . . it's a bit hard to get mis-quoted when you're answering the questions live on radio.

I must admit I was badly misquoted in a newspaper article after my second test match in which I managed to take six wickets for 15 runs against Pakistan at the Sydney Cricket Ground . . . I must have got them after a night out on the pork sandwiches!

Anyway when asked what it was like out in the middle, I explained something along the lines of, "It was easy having a bloke like Dennis Lillee bowling at the other end!"

Unfortunately for me, the newspaper heading next day read 'TEST CRICKET EASY — Max Walker'. Try explaining that one to your mates at work without appearing to be a bighead.

In many ways, speaking to the press can be similar to a visit to the dentist — you can just hope it's not gong to be a bad experience.

How does that story go about the frightened little boy in the dentist's chair? The drill operator in white says, "Just open wide, son and relax . . . trust me it'll be all right!"

Just as the whirrrr of the drill commences, a tiny arm reaches out from under the protective apron and grabs the dentist firmly on the testicles with a confident reply: "We're not going to hurt each other now, are we?"

It's a pity we can't grab some of those righteous columnists who sit in judgment and preach to the masses, without the right of reply.

And I suppose the bad luck award in my time occurred in Perth about six months before Kim Hughes' rebel cricketers toured South Africa for the first time.

Ian Brayshaw of ABC radio and I were to talk to South African administrator and power broker Ali Bacher (a former South African captain). The telephone hook-up was all set and everything worked out fine. Ali Bacher picked up the phone in Johannesburg as planned and we were away . . . a national scoop!

No-one else in Australia had spoken to Ali Bacher, the man who had a big say in making the rebel tour happen. He was speaking about safety, insurances, money, sponsors, attitudes — everything we wanted was being said.

The anticipation of the interview being networked Australia-wide was a satisfying thought. But by about six or seven minutes into our conversation the technician operating the master tape-recorder told us the worst — the tape recorder had not been recording. We could have cut our wrists!

All that we got was a few pleasantries and the fact that Mr Bacher was taking his daughter to university and couldn't speak any longer.

Yes, you get the good with the bad. So the next time you're watching TV or listening to radio, spare a thought for the person holding the microphone —it's not always as easy as it appears.

A Different Type of Crowd
'EVERY SECOND BLOKE HIT ME IN THE BELLY TRYING TO SHAKE HANDS'

It takes a lot of courage to stand up in front of a crowd of people and expect to entertain them by either speaking or singing. I've never attempted to sing for my supper, but I have been fortunate enough to see most of Australia through various speaking engagements.

They have ranged from the opal fields of Coober Pedy in Central Australia, to the tiny manganese mining settlement on Groote Eylandt in the Gulf of Carpentaria.

In many ways the first two or three minutes of any talk is a bit like bowling the first over of a Test match in front of a big crowd — it can really be a test of nerves!

You never quite know whether or not the new ball is going to swing; how the wicket will react; or, finally, whether the batsman is in a positive or negative frame of mind.

Audiences are no different . . . you've got to sum them up in the first two or three minutes! It's nice to know whether they like you or not early on . . . whether or not they want to laugh, or if they're purely interested in the information you can pass on.

The best way to break the ice is to get a laugh in the initial couple of minutes, usually at your own expense and it's not hard to verbally abuse ourselves, is it?

As a basic philosophy and guide to public speaking, I was told a long time ago to "tell 'em what you're gonna tell 'em, tell 'em and tell 'em what you've told 'em!"

It works pretty well too.

But, always be prepared for the unexpected situation that may arise.

A few years back I was asked to speak at a big dinner in the MCG members' dining room in Melbourne. I thought the function was to celebrate 100 years of competition between English and Australian blind cricketers. Much to my amazement, on arrival at the historic cricket venue, ready for the evening's formalities, I was told: "No, they aren't blind cricketers but deaf players." How do you think I felt?

Uncomfortable and edgy to say the least!

In the very excitable gathering were no less than 160 deaf players, plus wives and friends. A small contingent had even travelled all the way from England just to witness their own special Centenary Test Match.

Apart from the catering staff and barmen only three other people in attendance were able to hear 100 per cent. Some could lip read, a few could mouth the words but many could not!

Now for my talk. How was I going to get on? The manager of the English team was able to communicate verbally and the president of the Adult Deaf Society was fluent. Finally I had been given an interpreter to help me communicate with the masses.

My first mistake was to pick up the microphone: "Ladies and gentlemen . . .", but amidst a very loud and spontaneous roar of laughter I realised what I'd done — the microphone was absolutely useless.

Standing on a chair behind me was the interpreter translating everything I said through his magic-like fingers. At first, it was very off-putting because everyone's eye line was focused on this fellow's lightning fingers and not my face. Also the punch lines to all of my anecdotes were coming home about 45 seconds late.

I would be well and truly into a new story and the crowd would be only just reacting to the previous one. Anyway, I learned to live with it but, believe me, there was an enormous amount of nervous energy expended by both the interpreter and myself. Also, it was a hot, balmy night and before long the beads of perspiration were trickling down the side of my face.

Through the agency of my interpreter one of our English guests had the audacity to say that my accent was a bit off. Cheeky buggar!

But full points to the wonderfully talented man on the chair — my speech for the night was only ever going to be as good as his fingers. Public speaking is not only the choice of words, but also timing and inflection. He did all of these things with the movement and shape of his hands. He even created humour.

Some time later I did get to speak to a group of blind cricketers at their Blind Cricket Association presentation night. Again I felt quite humble.

Cricket is a difficult enough game with full use of both eyes, but to tackle the game of white flannelled gentlemen with less than 15 per cent sight available is a tribute to all of these courageous men.

I still treasure the 'blind cricket ball' — wicker woven ball with a bell in it —presented to me during their function.

Actually, many years before I did play in a blind cricket match at Mornington Peninsula. It was a fund-raising game including several Test cricketers — Dougie Walters and Gary Gilmour were two I remember.

We were allowed to bat for an over without the blinkers on — that was okay. But during our second over, talk about the blind leading the blind.

I don't know whether my hearing is poor or not, but I didn't have a clue where the hollow ball was coming from. Gary Gilmour wasn't much better. The local underarm quick bowler soon wrapped up 'Gus' with a bouncer that clanged against the metal stumps. A blind man's bouncer is a cunning delivery bowled underarm!

The game works this way. One of five players, with up to 15 per cent vision, points the bowler in the direction of the batsman. The bowler then shouts 'Ready John,' or whatever the batter's name is an away she goes rolling down the wicket.

The trick is to get the ball to jump or bounce awkwardly over the horizontal scraping technique of the batsman just as he swings at the ball. You'd be amazed how regularly a good bolwer can achieve it at a fair rate too!

At the presentation night, I was proud to be among such good people totally committed to playing the game.

Those with exceptional performances were rewarded with trophies. The only problem for me was handing them over. It was easy to get the trophy in a player's searching, outstretched hand but it was the other hand that was a worry. Every second bloke hit me in the belly trying to shake hands with the free one!

I managed a lot of laughs and a few claps at the end, so it made my night as well.

When you're talking to a live audience it's easy to know how you're going because of the feedback. Whatever we do in life we need feedback, either positive or negative.

In sport that feedback is spontaneous, hit a boundary or kick a goal and the spectators will roar with delight. Drop a catch or get hit for six, miss a goal or drop a mark and you'll be able to judge by the noise of the boos how badly you've performed.

It's exactly the same with a microphone in hand or lectern in front of you. Relate to the people you're talking to.

Remember, talk to your audience not at them, and their reaction to you will come back like a mirror image. They are all very important people too.

Speechless at the Office in the Sky

'IT SWAYED FROM SIDE-TO-SIDE — NO WONDER WE WERE SEASICK'

When driving rain and hailstorms stop play in a cricket match the players head for the safety and warmth of the locker room. For the commentators it's a matter of sitting tight until the bad weather blows over.

It was during one of these frustrating interruptions to play in Hobart during a McDonald's Cup match between Queensland and Tasmania that my fellow commentator Bill Lawry pointed out a thought-provoking

Bill Lawry: *bed sheet*   **Henry Blofeld: *nice drop***

possibility — not about the game but about the Channel 9 commentary team.

The man who uses a bed sheet for a handkerchief asked a question of yours truly and then answered it himself, "You know the most likely place for lightning to strike at this ground? . . . right here in the commentary position!

"We'd be cooked to a frazzle, like barbecued sausages . . . we wouldn't stand a chance!" he concluded.

He did have a point.

Here we were 10 metres above the ground behind the sightscreen in a prefabricated metal box supported by a scaffolding system constructed purely of rusty metal pipes. If ever there was a target for lightning it was our 'office' high in the sky!

Needless to say the weather dominated our conversations inside this building.

This trip to my tiny state of origin reminded me of the visit to Launceston the previous summer . . . and of course our position of vantage — not much different from the TCA ground in Hobart. Except that the door to the commentary box was a fridge type one with a similar handle. I'm sure our 'home' for the day must have been a deep freeze container in the past! Nevertheless, apart from being standing room only inside, it was warm enough for cool Tasmanian summer days.

Across to our right an even more primitive structure housed the eloquent English cricket commentator and journalist, the outspoken, Henry Blofeld who was working with Bill Jacobs on the Macquarie network.

They were both fine until rain began to make life very uncomfortable for them. Their only protection was a bright blue, waterproof tarpaulin which was primitively draped overhead.

Both orators were on their knees sheltering under the bench as 45 degree rain pelted through a gap in the canvas. Still, through all of these difficulties, the 'Blowfly' as he is affectionately known in Australia, had the composure to retain a long-stemmed glass of what looked like white of maturity, that is until he saw his image on the TV monitor doing just that!

Without spilling a drop of the good stuff, the articulate Pom popped the elegant glass back on the bench and continued speaking into his soggy microphone. His listeners wouldn't have been aware of the indulgence but millions of television viewers aren't blind. Nice drop Blowers old chap!

Things didn't improve much the next month in Adelaide for the inaugural day/night McDonald's Cup matches at Football Park.

South Australia played Queensland on the Saturday and lost, then Tasmania played the locals without success on Sunday. Both games were contested in cold and miserable conditions.

Grey, cumulo-nimbus clouds gathered above the state's best football venue and only a handful of spectators braved the bitter cold to see the history-making games!

Before any of the 'voices of cricket' could get a say, there was the small matter of a four-storey climb up an aluminium extension ladder.

Both ends were tied to the flimsy scaffolding structure with rope but still there remained much tolerance, not to mention the 60 kmh winds that gusted across the ground. Then consider climbing the narrow ladder, with a very heavy briefcase (laden with *Wisdens*) in one hand and the other blue from cold.

As I reached the platform area I could see the ABC commentary position — an open-air box. But at least the sight of the ABC staff, dressed in greatcoats, scarves and hats with just their blue noses and glowing cheeks uncovered, made me feel better. Inside our viewing location was an amazing colour scheme — purple carpeted walls, bright green floor and a white with gold fleck vinyl ceiling. Different.

This tiny metal-clad box was high above the field of play and fixed to the metal fascia of the grandstand by only two 50 mm diameter pieces of pipe. It swayed from side to side — no wonder we felt sea-sick after the first four hours.

Above us on the roof was a bank of cameras and their operators ... and boy do these fellas earn their money. Drenched to the back teeth, these cameramen have got to brave the worst conditions all day — and in the case of Adelaide, deep into the night.

In 1986 the Australian Cricket Board introduced an 'orange' cricket ball for day/night matches. From the start there were a few problems, especially for the camera guys who have to keep the ball on screen. Several of the chaps then had a problem picking up the orange ball on their viewfinders, which are black and white — the orange ball becomes the same dull grey tones as the grass!

Speaking of things not being easy to see ... halfway through a sentence during the South Australia v. Queensland game, one of the floodlights that help light the 'presenter' set crashed on to my head. It's the frist time I've been speechless for years!

Adelaide Oval is the normal venue for first class cricket in South Australia, and from the ABC commentary position, adjacent to the beautiful old scoreboard, it's a full day's entertainment just watching the people below.

It's amazing what 20 or 30 cups of warm beer and a solid dose of sunshine will do to a spectator.

The lads on the 'mini hill' love the not so modest young ladies who parade to and fro in front of the 'judges'. Many see the day at the cricket as total entertainment.

So when the cricket gets boring, which occasionally can happen, they judge the 'talent' on show. Needless to say the masses are pretty hard on some of the unsuspecting starters. For example the two fat girls in nipple pink, tight shorts . . . they scored a half and minus 1.

Then a policewoman in uniform attracted a sign stating 'Miss Piggy' another 'ET's Sister'. One young bikini-clad lass moving to the back of the crowd for no other reason than a call of nature, received a standing ovation and 11. On the way back the sign simply showed a huge pair of puckered lips.

The girls say they're embarrassed, yet deep down I'm sure they get a kick out of it all.

But back to the task of calling the cricket.

It can be a difficult problem sometimes to fluently pick up a player wearing coloured clothing and pronounce his name as if you've known him for years . . . particularly if he's an Indian or West Indian wearing a floppy hat, and his face is in shade! Unless they're smiling you just can't see 'em!

Like several commentators I was having a problem with Sunil Gavaskar, who must have changed the pronounciation of his name at least three times in the last decade.

So I selected what must have been the original version of Gavaskar . . . then it was pointed out to all of us by Richie Benaud that the correct way to call his name was 'Gavva-Skar'. Now that's fine if you've got a chance to think, but when a player drops a slip's catch it's very easy to slip back into the old pronounciation.

To give you an idea of the dry sense of humour possessed by the senior pro' Richie Benaud, before changing commentators, Richie said to me: "Big Max I think you'll find me a very patient man, but . . .!" And with no emotion on his face, other than a sparkle in the eye, he taped a sheet of foolscap bearing the phonetic spelling of the Indian opener's name — GAVVAR-SKAR!

I got the message but gee it's not easy!

Chapter Three

A BARREL OF LAUGHS FROM THE GREAT GAME

The streaker wanted to shake the great man by the hand.

Streaky Shot Claims The Master

'WE ALL GOT A LAUGH INCLUDING OUR CRESTFALLEN CAPTAIN'

G reg Chappell would agree that for him, playing matches against New Zealand hasn't been without its problems — for example the notorious underarm incident at the MCG.

Then, after our First Test debacle in 1985 — a loss by an innings and 41 runs in Brisbane — the Kiwis caused him a few more sleepless nights, this time as a national selector.

And I've still got very vivid memories of an incident during the 2nd Test match against New Zealand at Auckland in 1977.

Greg asked NZ to bat first on a rain-affected wicket at Eden Park. Australia exploited the difficult conditions to limit NZ to a first innings total of 229.

I'm sure our captain Greg Chappell was looking for a score of 350 plus and a lead of 150 on the first innings . . . and things were going nicely for our boys until just before tea on the second day.

It was an overcast day and a maximum temperature of about 5 degrees Celsius was forecast — I wonder how Tony Greig would read that against his 'player comfort' conditions on the Channel 9 weatherwall? Well anyway it was bitterly cold . . . even watching from the player's enclosure, as Rick McCosker and Greg both posted half centuries and Australia's total went beyond 150 for the loss of only one wicket.

Then it all started happening . . . a heavy dark cloud of smoke wafted across the ground from a house at the rear of the grandstand. It must have been serious because I remember the piercing shrill of a fire-engine ringing in my ears. As a batsman you really don't need that sort of interference with your concentration just as a bowler like Hadlee lets the ball go.

At the same time a streaker pranced out on to the rugby ground-cum-Test match venue, from the seated area in the northern section.

After jumping the fence and conducting a brief 'fashion' parade, he returned to his cheering audience. As he hopped the white picket fence, arms raised in triumph, I thought he might do himself an injury. No such luck. He regained his seat — still starkers.

With only a few minutes remaining before tea, NZ captain Glen Turner decided to give spinner Hedley Howarth a bowl. And while he was busy stepping out his run up, another well-sozzled streaker dashed across the ground from the northern end.

This bloke was 'well-dressed' though. He wore an impressive sun-tan, goose-pimpled bum, a pair of heavy boots, socks and a pale blue towelling hat. As he raced past the square leg umpire he flung his hat into the air and then disappeared over the wire gate at the southern end and into the carpark, hotly pursued by a policeman.

I could see both Greg and Rick getting more and more agitated by proceedings with the clock well past the time for the tea adjournment. All they wanted was to be NOT OUT at tea.

After just a couple of deliveries . . . streaker number one was back over the grass again.

So excited by the performance of master batsman Greg Chappell was he, the streaker wanted to shake the great man by the hand.

Incidentaly, he was sporting a pair of radio headphones so he could hear a blow by blow description of his antics.

He had bounded over the fence, evading Richard Hadlee at square leg, and continued lumbering towards our captain . . . who by this time was furious and staring glassy eyed at the naked man. His famous double scoop Gray Nicholls bat was raised above his head . . .

You see, Greg Chappell has never quite been the same about streakers after an incident in a Perth Shield match the previous year. Three women promptly paraded naked towards Greg and his not out partner.

From what Greg told me, one of them had beautiful eyes, though his mates tell me he wasn't looking at their eyes when he asked them to "hang around and have a chat".

But it all back-fired when the 'young lady' that Greg fancied turned out to be a female impersonator. He was shattered!

The whole thing had been a publicity stunt for a local night club — similar to the young blonde who bared it all in front of 100,000 people at a VFL grand final at the MCG a few years ago.

Since then it would be fair to say that streakers have never been his favourite people.

But back to New Zealand . . . in Greg's mind this bloke was jeopardising Australia' s aim of getting through the session without losing a wicket.

So Greg grabbed the man by his out-stretched hand and gave him a solid spanking across his polar bear white bottom . . . WHACK, WHACK, WHACK!!!

I can still hear these smacks now . . . an incredible sound.

Greg suggested he ". . . off!!!" And informed the man he was definitely not impressed. The streaker mentioned something about sticking the cord from his earphones in Greg's ear-holes. This brought about another couple of belts from the master's flashing bat!

By this time the policemen were in position and the offender was apprehended as he charged off.

The very next delivery, McCosker hit the ball to mid-on, but Chappell, thinking there wasn't a run in it, turned his back. Rick kept on running and was unfortunately run out at the striker's end by wicketkeeper Jock Edwards.

A disappointed Chappell left the field with his head hung low while the streaker was escorted out of the ground. Australia had now lost two wickets.

At stumps that night, Inspector George Dwan, one of the policemen who arrested the streaker, searched out Greg.

When the inspector entered the dressing room, everyone shut up, silence reigned supreme. He said: "Son, you ought to be ashamed of what happened out there!"

Greg replied: "Hang on a minute, you mean the streaker don't you?"

The policeman answered: "No, absolutely disgusting," with a certain sense of finality about the comment.

Greg looked blankly at the inspector and said, "Why?"

The answer is the moral to this story: "Here you are, you play four cross bat shots," illustrating with a movement of his arms as if to play a pull-shot, "when one straight drive would have done the trick!" And he followed through as if to play a big straight drive at an imaginary streaker!

Behind that serious expression then beamed an enormous smile and we all got a laugh including our crestfallen captain.

We won the match by 10 wickets, with almost two days remaining, thanks to some great bowling by Dennis Lillee who finished the match with figures of 11/123.

But one of my fondest memories of that match was standing at ninth slip. Yes ninth slip! Greg Chappell decided to use a 10-man slips cordon, including the wicker keeper Rodney Marsh.

Lillee was bowling to the worst No. 10 batsman I have ever seen in my life — a guy called Peter Retherick, a silver-haired off-spinner. It was an amusing tussle with such a field. But the terrified batsman held us up for about 40 minutes on the third day . . . long enough for us to have to come back after the rest day to take his wicket and then score the necessary 26 runs for victory.

Effectively he was at the crease for three days but he hardly hit a ball. Incredible. Well he can say he batted against Lillee for three days and I can say I fielded at ninth slip for Australia!

Funny what sticks in your mind during a Test match and that was my last against New Zealand.

A Short Exercise in being nice

'I GUESS THE SAFETY OF THE DRESSING ROOM MUST HAVE BEEN A TEMPTATION'

Looking back to the English summer of 1975, and the inaugural World Cup competition, it was not exactly a great time for Sri Lankan cricketers, and Sri Lankan batsmen in particular!

I'd never heard of some of their names, let alone know how to pronounce them. We thought they'd be a bit of a walkover and it certainly looked that way after we had scored 328 in the allotted 60 overs.

Then, between innings the fun really began to happen . . . in the Sri Lankan dressingroom. The atmosphere was very tense in their camp, mainly due to the fearsome reputations of Australia's two demon fast bowlers — Dennis Lillee and Jeff Thomson!

We Aussies were having quite a few problems too, but with the image as a team away from the ground. We were consequently dubbed the 'Ugly Australians' by the Fleet Street press gang.

Little did the Sri Lankans know that our boys had made up their minds to win some points back, as 'good guys' and decided to go easy on the 'novices'.

They didn't know that and when the two tiny opening batsmen emerged through the door into the bright sunlight . . they appeared to wince all the way to the wicket.

Dennis Lillee and Jeff Thomson opened the bowling for Australia at a very friendly pace and kept pitching the ball up into the blockhole or on the half volley. Sri Lanka were going along quite smoothly — no problems at all.

I thought our behavior was fantastic. We applauded their good strokes and we'd stop for a chat with the batsmen between overs to make them feel at home. No sign of the ugly Australian image now!

But when the score had reached 1/70, the public relations exercise had gone far enough. Chappelli, our captain, decided it was time for a few wickets — and quickly.

That little instruction was like a red rag to a bull . . . Dennis the Menace couldn't help himself and was soon in danger of bruising his big toe, so short was he bowling! Whilst at the other end Thommo got real nasty and really quick.

With one delivery Thommo hit opening batsman S. Wettimuny right on the top of his front foot — it was a fearful blow.

Wettimuny at this stage had been untroubled in making 53 excellent runs. But this crushing blow to the foot at about 95 mph made the slightly built righthander drop his bat and limp beyond the square leg umpire before he fell to the ground in agony. Was it a broken toe?

The idea of 'retired hurt' — 53, against his name on the scoreboard was not altogether unappealing. And I guess the safety of the dressing room must have been a big temptation to the man. Nevertheless the captain down at the non-striker's end, wouldn't hear of it. "Bat on like a man!" he said.

It was a strange sight, the front foot carefully cradled on top of the back sandshoe. He looked like a one-legged stork fishing in shallow water. I thought the wind on the next delivery was going to blow him off balance as it passed his right earhole!

Two balls later Thomson struck again. Same batsman. Same toe.

This time the little Wettimuny S. really wanted out. He'd suffered enough.

"No." ordered his skipper, "bat on!"

Bravely, Wettimuny faced the next Thomson delivery. Similar ball. Same result. Same toe.

Unfortunately it wasn't three direct hits and you're out! He tried desperately to occupy the crease for just one more delivery with that throbbing toe supported on the arch of his back foot, which had crept slowly back to the base of the middle stump, obviously to give himself more room to play Thommo.

This was all very well but the sight of the blond fast bowler vigorously chewing his gum and slowly polishing the red cherry by gyrating his pelvis proved just too much.

The little opener overbalanced completely. He shouted the word, "I go off, I go off!" loudly out to his captain who was still peering over his shoulder to see if Thommo was on his way.

So, nursing the most tormented toe in the history of first-class cricket our friend convinced his captain that fighting for his country was all very well, but being crippled was a bit bloody rough. Or words to that effect — he was speaking very quickly as Sri Lankans do when they're excited or frightened! He may have been frightened!

Wettimuny, 53 not out, hobbled unassisted for the first 50 yards back to the pavilion, then was propped up by two team-mates for the next 30 yards. To a standing ovation he fell through the dressingroom door, just before the next man in, Duleep Mendis, was shoved out of the safety of that same dressingroom.

Mendis became captain of his country but in this game all he had going for him was a pounding heart inside his small but robust frame.

But the gutsy little Sri Lankan surprised us all. He played some sensational cover drives on his way to 32 and was just getting settled. Then, just a few balls later a Thomson 'kicker' reared nastily off a good length, glanced off Mendis' glove and hit him dead centre, right between the eyes!

Mendis collapsed. I thought Thomson had killed the guy . . . as it turned out, not quite!

My mate Thommo always had this terrific knack of getting the cricket ball to roll back down the wicket towards him after he'd hit a batsman. It didn't matter whether it was the thigh, ribs or head — the ball used to still roll slowly down the pitch towards him. He reckoned it saved him having to follow through too far!

Well that's exactly what happened on this occasion . . . Thomson quickly picked up the rolling ball and looked to throw the batsman's stumps down for the run out.

The run out wasn't on though because despite having fallen forward, the batsman still had both feet behind the batting crease and had his chin deeply embedded in the surface of the pitch.

Now what would any sport-loving fast bowler do in this same situation? See whether the victim would like any help.

Thommo was just about to grab the poor fellow by the scruff of the neck and turn him over when he too said "I go off now, I go off!" We were just glad to hear him speak. Naturally we called for a stretcher.

And I thought I'd seen everything but what happened next takes the cake! The KO'd batsman got up, ran 30 yards towards the stretcher bearers and hopped straight on. He was then carried off to an enormous roar from a majority Pakistan and Indian contingent in the crowd . . . he even waved goodbye!

Thomson copped a lot of outrage and criticism in the press over the incident and for his "wanting to see blood on the wicket comment" made prior to the tour.

Today I take my hat off to the small country of Sri Lanka because in the big bad world of international cricket they've come a long way since that forgettable game in 1975.

An Old Cobbler to the rescue
'SOMETIMES SPORTSMEN FORGET ABOUT LOGIC IN THEIR ENDEAVOR FOR SUCCESS'

What's so special about a much-loved and well-worn pair of old cricket boots? In many ways everything! They're a sort of security system —when my feet feel good, I feel good!

A brand new pair of cricket boots straight off the sports store shelf probably will have great arch supports, popular screw-in sprigs, snow white leather uppers and extra long laces that are guaranteed not to break, for a while.

But they'll also be very stiff with an unfamiliar feel — like total strangers — and be unbalanced.

Naturally, it takes time for them to feel comfortable and finally to become the best of friends! And I know all boots start out with an unbecoming odor.

Generally it takes either a lot of miles at practice, or an extraordinary personal success on the playing field, before they're ultimately given the nod as a pair of good'ns! . . . and with a score on the board it's easy to look forward to the next outing in what have become lucky boots.

I'm not really superstitious but if I took wickets in a pair of boots then it was always my belief that there were plenty more where they came from.

Mind you it can work in reverse — no more wickets, no more boots. Time to break in the new ones!

A desperate player will try anything to get a wicket. I managed to have great respect for several pairs of warped and dirty old boots during my career spanning 13 years . . . some almost rotted at the seams, caused by extremely sweaty feet.

One pair consistently needed a 75 mm wide strip of elastoplast bandage to prevent the sole from competely pulling away from the upper. In other words the boot was only as strong as the tape! That had to be upgraded before every session of play. Really it was an impractical solution, but sometimes sportsmen forget about logic in their endeavor for success.

It was always the running-in period that proved the most painful, and on many occasions the difference between acceptance or not, occurred very early in the boot's life. After all if you can't stand up because your footwear hurts, then you might as well forget about bowling a stint of 25 overs and taking five wickets. Your focus will be on the pain and not the task of removing batsmen.

One of the most common problems with cricket boots was the design of the sprigs or spikes and especially their placement.

Being a big bloke and pretty heavy on my feet, I needed more than the average fast bowler. I discovered that the screw-in variety very quickly formed painful corrugations in the sole because the diameter of the flat flange supporting the female socket, which accepts the threaded sprigs, was not quite wide enough. Consequently hurtful little lumps grew in the leather sole and more so in a plastic one.

Imagine having 13 of these little inverted volcanoes probing the soles of your feet . . . on wickets of hard baked clay it feels like nothing short of walking on a bed of blunt, hot nails.

I overcame this problem by getting my boots hand-made by a fascinating old bootmaker named Hope Sweeney — a legend in the sports footwear business. A master at stitching up lightweight footy boots, athletes' spikes and cricket boots.

The first time I met Hope he had his arms full of boots. It was in the MCG members' car park — the old cobbler was delivering some custom-made kangaroo hide boots to the great Dennis Lillee, during a Sheffield Shield match between Victoria and Western Australia.

After successfully fitting the fiery fast bowler with his magnificent new boots, he came next door into the Victorian dressing room to have a closer look at my not-so-pretty feet, including the three dead toe nails.

The silver-haired, bespectacled old craftsman soon produced two foolscap-size cardboard backings from the old maroon vinyl travel bag he was carrying on his shoulder.

I stood barefooted on each piece of cardboard while Hope carefully traced the outline of each foot, including my hammer-head shaped big toes to form a template of the sole.

Then he asked if he could have a pair of well-worn boots I didn't need. Gee I only had two pairs in those days . . . so I was loath to let them go, but from those old faithfuls he could expertly judge just which areas needed special attention, extra strength or building up.

Such was the quality and demand for his work, Hope had a waiting list of up to two years, but seeing I was a mate of Dennis Lillee's must have helped me up the 'batting' order. Just a matter of weeks later I got to try on this magnificent pair of boots — I'd never experienced anything quite like this before.

Honestly, they were like kid gloves on the feet and I felt as if I'd been wearing them all season. From that point on in 1976 I was hooked.

Anything else could not compare with the old-timer's wonderful craftsmanship. It was blatantly obvious why top players from right around the world waited, sometimes for years, for a pair of his boots. No more standard boots for me! No way!

Each heel had a nice chunky wedge of black rubber built into it to absorb the impact of my clumsy, tangled feet pounding up and down on hard pitches, especially in the violent delivery stride.

In the past, before I met Mr Sweeney, I'd gone to great lengths to prevent getting a jarred heel — not always successfully. And anyone who has ever suffered from this type of injury would agree, it is not an easy one to carry through an afternoon of bowling . . . but at times I had to!

One of the more exotic techniques I used to overcome the pain, was to cut an orange in half and after squeezing out some of the juice, I would place it in the troublesome boot heel. It might sound a bit odd, but believe me it did work — even if a little squelchy under foot. There was plenty of vitamin C for the boot but I'm pretty sure the orange juice didn't do the inside of the boot much good. One had to be very careful not to get a healthy outcrop of mould appearing.

The other solution to the problem was to use a high-jumper's plastic heel-cup, inside the sock, hard up against the flesh. These didn't last very long — maybe a few overs — but were great in the short term. The problem was changing the cracked plastic cups during play.

Any amount of foam rubber was experimented with, but without too much success. The foam used to compress into a tiny hard ball and the result was even more pain than without any form of cushion.

Another method was to pinch my wife's thongs and cut them in half — but thanks to Hope Sweeney divorce was averted.

Secrets of the Willow

'GRAPES, ORANGES AND PAPER CUPS RAINED ON MY BACK FOR ABOUT THREE MINUTES'

The world's best bruiser of Kookaburra cricket balls, Viv Richards, and I don't have much in common. As an athlete, the West Indies captain has the pace of a gazelle on heat, whereas my nickname is appropriately 'Tanglefoot'.

Viv was born in Antigua, a tiny island in the Caribbean, whilst my pedigree stems from Tasmania.

Despite such differences, not to mention the obvious one — the ability to handle a piece of willow successfully — we both used to use the same brand of cricket bat — Stuart Surridge. Well that was before Duncan Fearnley made Viv an offer too good to refuse . . . and in pounds sterling, too!

Anyway just what is so special about a cricket bat — the feel, the look, the smell (and they do smell), the name?

I think far and away the most important thing about a cricket bat is that it should make runs, no matter who uses it.

Everyone can remember their first cricket bat — I got mine from Father Christmas at the innocent age of seven after I sent him a letter addressed to the North Pole.

Obviously Santa wasn't too special at choosing what was good and what was bad. It must have cost my old man no more than 30 shillings in those days — a sickly looking bleached piece of Kashmir willow (maybe a piece of fence paling).

I can still remember standing it in a nugget tin top of linseed oil overnight and finding the bottom swollen beyond recognition the next day.

Several weeks later I realised it wasn't a piece of willow . . . I was getting out too often! It wasn't long before I began banging in the stumps with the face of the bat . . boys don't do it because it's really not good for the bat. And what about the three pieces of filler that fell out of my piece of 'plank'!

Bats vary a great deal in weight. Both Greg and Ian Chappell were great believers in the heavy bludgeoning timbers — around 2lb 12oz to 3lb.

The 'Super Cat' Clive Lloyd took this further to about 3lb 5oz and as well as the weight, he added three or four rubber grips to make the handle larger.

Ian Botham displayed how devastatingly good a heavy piece of English willow can be, when waved in anger — he took 22 runs off a Merv Hughes over, during the First Test at the Gabba during the 1986-87 tour, to post one of the most exciting hundreds I've ever seen in Test cricket!

But let me tell you how Clive Lloyd got me one night during Kerry Packer's cricket revolution.

Australia were locked in a tense struggle with the West Indies . . . who needed to score at about 14 runs an over with five overs remaining.

The terms of floodlighting VFL Park, Glen Waverley, came under a local council ruling that demanded the lights go out at precisely 10.30 p.m. That night, I was never so pleased to see the lights go out — after bowling only four balls in the over the giant West Indian batsman had sent two massive hits way over the rope for sixes and two blistering drives on either side of the wicket for four. I was able to walk off the ground, my embarrassment hidden by the darkness.

The West Indies won the game on a run rate . . . so as you can see it can happen to the best of us. Even the great Dennis Lillee had 44 taken off only four overs by the tiny left hander, Alvin Kallicharan, during the World Cup preliminaries in 1975 at the Oval.

Clive Lloyd: *three or four rubber grips*

I was standing at fine leg getting a sunburnt roof of the mouth as I watched several hook shots disappear over my head and into the crowd.

The excitable crowd of calypso brothers kept shouting at me, "Why doesn't he bowl the bouncer now, man?"

My reply upset them even further when I explained that in Australia we didn't bowl bouncers at unrecognised batsmen. Grapes, oranges and paper cups rained on my back for about three or four minutes until I picked up a bunch of grapes and began eating them!

When I first arrived in Melbourne way back in 1967 to pursue a career in cricket and football; as well as to study architecture, I became great friends with the chairman of selectors of the Melbourne Cricket Club, Clive Fairbairn. He ran a thriving sports goods business in Little Bourke Street.

Many successful sporting people in Melbourne were given a start with some 'free' gear and kind words of encouragement from Clive but in my case he added, "The way you bat, this one will last you about 10 years!"

Still, I accepted that 'Rapier' bat autographed by Bill Lawry.

The old-fashioned cricket bat needed lots of care . . . today some of the pre-finished plastic coated and painted varieties are supposedly ready for immediate use.

As a teenager I used to sleep with my bat close to the bedhead so I could look at it and dream of far away achievements — I know some kids even sleep with the bat inside the blankets.

A new cricket bat demanded much tender loving care to bring it to peak performance. First a light sanding to make the surface more able to absorb the oil from the smelly old rag that followed the sandpaper up and down the face. Some schools of thought suggest that seven parallel grains in the willow is the ultimate, others say five . . . I didn't even mind if the face had a big ugly knot or 'butterfly' somewhere near the sweet spot.

Then there was the use of pigskin to hold the bat together . . . it was almost like a status symbol in my early days. If a bat had pigskin on it then it must have scored a lot of runs.

A new bat used to be left overnight horizontal with the maker's name or face looking at the ceiling.

Next exercise was to put a well-worn leather cricket ball into an old sock and suspend it from the clothes-line on a piece of string. Then gently "play" the bat in with forward and back defensive shots against the pendulum action of the swinging sock.

The future development of the conventional cricket bat was helped when Ian Chappell became the first player to use the radically designed 'scoop' bat in a Test match. This practice of scooping out a larger amount of the meat or weight in order to keep the edges thicker and gaining a larger sweet spot, has now been refined by Gray Nicholls with much success.

When Dennis Lillee agreed to use his aluminium cricket bat in a Test match shock-waves rippled across the WACA ground as England captain Mike Brearley protested on the grounds of the bat damaging the ball.

It was a strange design of simple ribs fixed to a central pipe or handle around which aluminium facing was wrapped.

The early varieties of the bat had a gaping hole on the toe that constantly filled up with dirt . . . Dougie Walters discovered it was a great place to butt his cigarettes.

Actually Dougie Walters proved the big heavy bat theory wrong . . . Dungog Dougie used only a 2lb 5oz bat and was one of the game's biggest hitters.

So was I if I ever got one in the middle. All too often it was the middle stump that disappeared and not the ball. I blame the bat!

This game was a riot

'SOME OF HIS TEAM-MATES HAD BEEN BETTING ON 20 YEARS WITH HARD LABOR'

Fear is an incredible feeling but I doubt if I've ever been so frightened as during the riot at Georgetown, Guyana during the 1979 World Series Cricket tour of the Caribbean.

During the course of the riot, which only lasted 45 minutes, $60,000 worth of damage was done — terrifying in fact! We were a long way from home and had nowhere to go!

Finally the rioting finished, thanks to the arrival of the militia at the ground, complete with their perspex shields, sub-machineguns, truncheons and tear-gas. What a relief!

Nearly an hour had passed without further violence and by that time we were all looking like wrung out wet rags. I'm sure most of us could have got through two or three eight ounce rum punches without much effort.

We quickly realised that whilst we were enjoying the respite, the violent mob were taking the chance to regroup along the route, which we would have to take, in order to get back to the hotel where we were staying!

So another way home had to be found and was. Back at the hotel — more militiamen. There were four of them, with the inevitable sub-machineguns.

On the 4th floor of the hotel we found another reception committee — four plain clothes policemen with colt 45s under their armpits. They were playing cards. Even Doug Walters didn't want to play a hand or two with them. He reckoned the stakes were too high!

Later that evening, the Australians had a team meeting where much common sense was in evidence. We voted 14-3 to catch the next plane home! At that stage, we were not aware of the Ian Chappell drama that was to develop a couple of days later.

Ian became involved in an incident with local official Insun Ali — a blow to the stomach was mentioned — and the publicity gained him no friends in Georgetown.

But back to our vote — the decision didn't stand. We were given some advice by local officials to the effect that we should consider playing some cricket or we might never get out of Guyana!

We were reminded, pointedly, of the bloodstains that marked the place where two CIA men had died after coming from the U.S. to check on the Jonestown Affair. There wasn't much more discussion, just another vote which decided we would play a mini-Super Test in the two days remaining of the original match, plus the rest day.

It is always an honor to be named in a cricket team. No-one likes to be left out, or named 12th man. But this was a slightly different proposition —different enough for me to be extremely pleased to draw the 12th man spot!

Gary Gilmour was even happier to be 13th man and big Mick Malone celebrated his 14th man position by not leaving the hotel for three days straight! How he survived on the curried horse or goat they gave him to eat I'll never know.

The match started on time, and I have never been involved in one like it before and hope never to repeat such an experience. Cricket is a game where concentration is all important. Even fielding at third man the mind has to be completely free of any other worries. That day all the players were on edge. One and three-quarter eyes were on the crowd — the ball was watched with whatever was left.

Of course, I had the easy job of serving drinks. It was even easier than usual because two of the local lads had volunteered to get them ready for me. There were two large plastic jugs of water and the boys were busy emptying the little bottles of Coca-cola into the third. I busied myself ladling the Staminade into the water.

"I stir it for you, Mr Walker", one of the lads suggested. Grateful for the help, I nodded and turned to put the Staminade jar back in its place. As I turned back again, the lad was just lifting his arm out of the second jug. It had never occurred to me that he wouldn't use a spoon! The drink was dripping from his arm, over the scabs of seven or eight sores!

It was good fortune that Australia was batting . . . I didn't think I would have much trouble persuading our batsmen not to drink the Staminade. Those members of the team who had not been struck with a dose of Montezuma's Revenge before the riot, sure had a king-sized attack after it!

I pushed the trolley out to the centre and stood chatting with Trevor Chappell and Martin Kent, handing out the batting hints and generally being helpful. "You're doing a great job lads (we were 1/26 at the time). All you've got to do is hold in there till lunch and we'll win this match."

"Don't know about that Tangles, I'd soon as be out next ball", young Trevor said, giving me the impression that he wasn't all that happy. I asked him what was wrong — and got an answer I hadn't been expecting.

"Don't make it too obvious what you're doing, Tang, but have a look at that white-washed building behind the grandstand. Can you see that window on the second floor with the wooden louvres?"

I turned around, trying hard to make the gesture look casual. "I can see it, but what's the matter? There isn't any glass, so it can't be glinting in your eyes."

"It's not," he replied, "but there's a bloke in there who keeps bobbing up and down with something in his hands. Now if he's got a rifle with one of those telescopic sights . . . and if he looks at the scoreboard and mistakes 'T. Chappell' for 'I Chappell' . . . Here Trevor paused to let the idea sink into my skull. "I'm as good as dead, aren't I?" he finished.

I had to agree with him — and that is an indication of how jumpy we were. Now that Trevor had made the point, I could feel the hairs on the back of my neck standing up every time I thought about that sniper's nest.

I promised him it would be checked out immediately and headed back to the pavilion. Joking about someone getting shot, as we had the previous night, was one thing; standing out there at the crease with the thought that the back of your head was filling someone's telescopic sights, was an entirely different matter.

It eventuated that the man in the room was just a keen cricket fan, taking advantage of his position to watch the game through binoculars. Another of those incidents that cause a laugh when recalled now, but at the time it was deadly serious. And I mean deadly.

The match itself fizzled out to a draw — there was never going to be time enough for any other result.

And that, we fondly thought, was the end of the fun and games in Guyana. Again, we were wrong, and M. Walker in particular had problems. I was scheduled to return to Australia well before the rest of the team, so I could be with my wife Tina for the birth of our second child.

Getting out of Georgetown presented something of a problem. People who say there is a lot of red tape involved in getting in and out of Australia don't know the half of it. Exit from Georgetown requires a ticket, a passport, and, of all things, a tax clearance certificate. The last item is to make sure people don't skip the country until they have paid their income tax; the piece of paper says no money is owed to the Government.

But I had an even bigger problem at that moment — I didn't even have a passport. And my captain Ian Chappell was mixed up in that little matter, which went back to the riotous Super Test.

He was being sued for assault and just about everything else the legal people could dream up. Mr Ali had to move fairly smartly, as it wasn't the intention of us Aussies to stay around in Guyana once the match was over.

Such are the vagaries of the Guyanese legal system that we all had our passports confiscated. It appeared as if they were determined that one of us was to be shot — and it didn't really matter which one! Presumably their thinking was that if Ian decided to make a break for freedom by swimming through shark-infested waters back to Australia, the penalty could be extracted from the rest of us, still stranded there without our passports!

Ian was lucky. He was fined only $100 while some of his team-mates had been betting heavily on 20 years with hard labor.

Getting my passport back so that I could leave when I needed to was going to take fast-talking and persuasive string-pulling. The fact that I had no part in the incident relating to the court case, and that I wanted to be home for the birth of my second child, didn't cut any ice with local officials.

I don't know who worked the miracle, but to whoever it was, I was most grateful. Eventually I made it home and only when you have been through something similar to that do you realise how good it was to get back to the relative quiet of Bay 13.

A Pilgrimage to Mecca

'I JUST TACKED MYSELF ON TO THE END OF THE LINE'

To visit Lord's, or the home of cricket as they would have it believed in England, would have to be one of the high points in the life of anyone who is even remotely interested in the game.

Even as a young boy in my formative years, I was obsessed by the great game of cricket — I dreamed of one day proudly wearing the baggy green cap on to the sacred turf at Lord's.

My early recollections of cricket's holy of holies were the wonderfully descriptive word pictures of the great commentators, men like John Arlott, the unforgettable Englishman and the ABC's Alan McGilvray.

The static crackle of the short wave radio band added a sense of curiosity and magic to the gentleman's game as the score came to us from the other side of the world in the night.

Gee, it was really great to return to England again in 1985 for the fourth occasion — the attraction being the ultimate Lord's Test match, England v Australia.

This time I took a party of cricket-loving Australians to the Mecca of our white flannelled fools — it'll still be a while before the English establishment can cope with bright lights, white balls and colored gear! Here at Lord's the game has stood still for almost 200 years apart from the onset of one-day cricket.

During the first day at Lord's, the Australian team's dressing room balcony seemed a great place to hang the touring team's major sponsor banner — XXXX Castlemaine beer. The reaction from the people who count was: "No cricket while the sign remains!" Needless to say the sign fell to floor level very abruptly . . . and cricket continued as usual between MCC and Australia.

The excitement of the first day at any Test match is always intense, but coping with another 30 odd people must have got the better of me, because I was the only member of our busload of Aussies to forget his ticket!

With so much talk of security problems and fire hazards at sporting events these days I thought, "Gee, I'm really going to have to be a silver-tongue today if I'm going to gain entry to the ground, let alone get a seat!"

Well, no problem at the main gate — I just explained to the little MCC official entrusted with the job of not letting blokes like me in without a ticket, that my name was Max Walker and I had a group of 35 people with me from Australia. But it didn't mean anything to him!

Nevertheless, he did help me count them through the large black wrought iron gates . . . 34, 35 and I just tacked myself on to the end of the line and said, "Thanks mate!" with a broad Australian accent.

Then came a lonely thought: "Everyone else has got somewhere to sit except me, and the first ball is just half an hour away. Will I get through the next two checkpoints into the Mound Stand seating area?"

The same old trick worked beautifully on the guy guarding entry to the rear of the Mound Stand via the dirty grey committee staircase.

Now for the big one — the bull-necked man with the MCC official badge proudly fixed high on his left lapel looked like a bloodhound on the scent —very efficient! I watched him seat several of my party, but not before he ran his eagle eye across each ticket stub, marked area "M", the area within his jurisdiction, and pointed to the seat number.

One deep breath and half a flight of stairs brought me face to face with the elderly, bespectacled gentleman. I'm sure he could sense the anxiety within me.

I told him quietly that one of those vacant seats down there between where we were standing and the playing area belonged to me, but since I'd forgotten my ticket it was difficult to say which one. His reply in a strong Cockney accent was, "Yeah, they all say that . . . someone else has paid good money for them there seats and it ain't you!"

Desperate, I thought I should get a bit heavier, so I told him again who I was, former Test player, honorary life member of the MCC and all that good strong stuff. His answer to all that was, "Yeah, yeah . . . well if you're a bloody member why ain't you in the members' stand, instead of wasting time out 'ere?"

He did have a point though! Defeated and dejected, I slowly pushed my way back down the stairs as about 50 pairs of 'Pommie' eyes silently rejoiced at my lack of success. That was the only success they had that day, though.

Ultimately the problem was solved by using one of the younger members of the tour — Alistair Lord, just 11 years old. I used his ticket to get past my conscientious MCC official while he ran the gauntlet by diving backwards and forwards past the security.

The game itself is history how — a great victory for Australia including some memorable performances. Notably the 196 and 41 not out by captain courageous, Allan Border, as he slowly but surely warmed to the responsibility of leading his country.

Yes, it was worth the effort of travelling almost 10,000 miles to witness that contest . . . and also to run into some old friends. Most of these were met at the Australian Trade Tent at the Nursery end of the ground.

Freddie Trueman was one of the first to make himself known to us; I suppose it's because Freddie's not shy! He couldn't let me return to Australia without a couple of his 'gems'.

I asked him whether he really liked West Indians or whether it was just a rumour. He said, "Yes, but I doubt if I could eat a whole one!"

The other question I put to him was: "How come you play cricket so late at night over here?" His answer to this one was, "Geez Maxie, if only we could get rid of all the Pakistanis in Yorkshire we'd probably be able to play for another hour and a half — they don't reflect much light you know!"

He's always good value for a laugh or two. Keith Miller was there too for the 40-year reunion of players who played in the famous 'Victory Tests' immediately after the war. So too were Linday Hassett and Ray Lindwall.

Freddie Titmus, the English off-spinner, who unfortunately lost his big toe in a water-skiing accident while touring the Caribbean, is still limping and I must say still drinking.

Also 'Wag' the chief security officer for Australia House in London was still on duty, beautifully uniformed, outside the trade tent. At £50 a ticket a day, his job was to stop intruders who weren't bona fide guests! There's barely an Australian Test cricketer during the past 25 years who hasn't crossed this man's path — one of the great characters of Lord's.

What would a visit to Lord's be without a souvenir or a visit to the Museum? We did one better — a guided tour of the Long Room — the room in the members' grandstand that houses so many pinstriped suits, much cigar smoke and those ghastly MCC members' ties, all egg yolk and ketchup. You wouldn't wear one for a bet but they really are plentiful at Lord's.

Our not so charismatic guide, joked about the rows of bentwood chairs fronting the huge clear glass windows to the ground. "Very comfortable even though they don't look it, but great for keeping an eye on who's asleep in front of you!" he said smirking in agony at the tiled floor. I wouldn't recommend he leave his day job to be a comedian.

Actually the floor was quite fascinating — millions of tiny sprig marks punctured by nervous batsmen making their way to the wicket through the masses of members.

Finally before our eyes in the museum was that tiny urn called 'The Ashes.' It didn't seem to be the sort of trophy that countries would risk life and limb for but there it was, a tiny brown piece of pottery with some poetic words inscribed on the front.

The Domination of the Bat
'THE SURFACE OF THE WICKET REMAINS SUPER SMOOTH'

I always thought cricket was a batsman's game! That's spoken from the heart of one of the foundation members of the bowlers' union. But you can't tell me that a run feast and bowlers fielding at fine leg is the sort of cricket that spectators want to see.

The problem is for the authorities; people want to watch a good contest and with too few wickets falling they don't get it.

Fans want results — no one wants to go and watch a drawn Test match where average batsmen dominate every innings.

I may sound like a retired medium pacer with an old ball in hand, pushing off the sightscreen for my 30th consecutive over in 35 degree heat. But any fair dinkum Australian cricket lover would agree, it's hardly the sort of 'contest' to promote our great game, or more particularly, to try and regain the public's support.

Yes, the game of cricket is in danger of deteriorating into a batsman's game, at the expense of some of my colleagues; the pacemen, spinners and most significantly the pitches.

Well, one of the most fashionable theories blames the batsman's cricket boots. Not bad, eh? Blame the poor old batsman again?

But really, I see it as a very valid reason for the dominance of the willow over the red ball. The theory is that batsmen who choose to wear rubber-sole shoes don't dig up the pitch as they occupy the crease.

They might sound OK but instead, they destroy the grass in and around the batting crease, as well as in areas where they run and skid.

Now this makes grass regrowth impossible for the next game and consequently, as the season progresses, the quality of wickets deteriorates.

But just as important — during the course of the match — the surface of the wicket remains super smooth, almost like glass and this handicaps the bowlers. Many of the quicker bowlers reckon the ball merely skids on to the batsmen with no variation in cut or seam.

Similarly, the spin bowlers also have to contend with this smooth surface throughout the game as at no stage does the wicket crumble to become suitable for spin.

The ideal wicket for a four day contest is help for the fast men on day one, a batting paradise on days 2-3, and taking spin on the final day.

The solution to our very serious problem is to force all batsmen to wear spikes — at least on the ball of their footwear.

It's funny how the pendulum swings. Remember more than a decade ago, when John Benaud was suspended from Shield cricket for wearing rubber, ripple sole shoes? He's the culprit. After he got his way, everybody began to wear a variety of rubber soled footwear.

One of our Test match curators, Les Burdett, of the picturesque Adelaide Oval, is quite outspoken about the problem. He believes that sprigs would solve most of our problems in this area.

"If all first class batsmen wore spiked shoes, it would help balance the ledger as it did in the old days," he said.

"There would be a natural wear on the wicket. This would mean the wicket should assist spinners more as the match progressed, and surely that is what the natural development of a match should be.

"It also would help pacemen. As the pitch wore, it would crack more than it does these days and provide variation.

"And of course, from a curator's view point, it would mean the natural break-up of the pitch would enable the grass to grow back quickly so that good wickets could be produced for the next match."

Les ought to know and the Adelaide Oval curator went on to say that the effect of a ruling in South Australia grade cricket in 1982 backs up his argument.

"Grade players have been forced to wear spiked shoes for the past three seasons — or they are fined $25 — and the games have become more balanced between bat and ball, and the standard of wickets has improved remarkably," he said.

At the other end of this hallowed piece of turf, many batsmen refute the argument by saying they prefer the comfort of rubber-soled shoes.

My opinion is that it is definitely more hazardous batting in rubbers on wet wickets or crumbling pitches. Most first class batsmen do have boots with sprigs in them anyway, so why not unload the rubber soled version? Save them up for when they retire to Sunday afternoon cricket in the park on the concrete slabs — that's when you need them!

Towards the end of my career, during the late 70s, bowlers suffered a few setbacks at the hands of the almighty batsman. It was said that pacemen during those years held an extraordinary advantage due to the thick 'cat gut' stitching on the seam of the ball — it ensured prodigious movement.

I can honestly tell you under a clear blue sky at the MCG on a flat track, there was definitely no movement — in fact mostly it was gun-barrel straight!

So, that astute national selector and former Test all-rounder, Sam Loxton, assessed the situation in 1978 and, naturally, he had the seam flattened!

Maybe, that's one of the reasons why today we have no Bob Massie's on the scene, let alone batsmen wearing spikes.

I wonder sometimes just how far our game has progressed, if at all: coloured gear, white ball and day/night competition.

Gee, in my day I only had one pair of boots and they were heavy leather soled bowling boots with heaps of long metal sprigs. So I bowled in them as well as batted — mind you I never suffered from over-exposure at the crease.

There was one exception in 1977 during our ill-fated tour of England under Greg Chappell's captaincy. In the final Test at The Oval Mick Malone and myself posted a century partnership (102) before Mick left the scene, just before lunch.

Dickie Bird was the umpire on that occasion. And in his wisdom, while I was batting along comfortably — and with the score against my name reading 42 not out — he ordered me to leave the ground to replace my heavy bowling boots with rubber-soled shoes.

As I passed him I said: "Dick, you think I'm running up and down this wicket so that I'll bowl you Poms out in the second innings, don't you?"

Before the eccentric little umpire with the white golf hat could answer, I chipped in with: "Well you're wrong, 'cos I'm going to make a hundred in a Test match today!"

He grinned cheekily and said: "That is balderdash!"

Unfortunately he was right . . . I got 78 not out, when I ran out of partners. Another hundred nipped in the bud!

I didn't bat any better in rubbers — actually I found it more difficult turning, because of lack of traction, although I did have a turning circle like the QEII.

I wonder what Dickie Bird would do today? Let me stay and assist the 'natural wear and tear' on the wicket?

Derring-do of the Autograph Hunter

'THEY WERE NICE ENOUGH TO SAY THEY REMEMBERED THE INCIDENT'

Money can't buy the look on a child's face the moment a sportsman accepts to sign his or her autograph book. True magic. In 1985, it was an autograph hunters paradise because 28 Test captains from around the world had gathered to celebrate the centenary of Test cricket at the Adelaide Oval.

The events away from the playing fields were very festive, especially the Centenary Test dinner, held at the Hilton Hotel, after the completion of the third Test match against the West Indies the previous month.

For some 600 guests, that night was also the chance of a lifetime to collect some of the greatest names ever to grace a cricket scoreboard.

The legends themselves stood up well, after some five hours or more of constant signing.

Understandably, for the likes of Sir Donald Bradman, 75, resilient Englishman Gubby Allen, 82, and many other senior gentlemen, the evening must have been a great strain. Yet, they never once lost their composure in a sea of extended autograph books and menus — soon to become family heirlooms.

This was very refreshing, as some of our contemporary sportsmen and women obviously do not realise the enormous good a smile and or a signature can do especially for a young kid's development.

And after all, even if there isn't time to sign his book or crumpled piece of paper, as is so often the case, it costs nothing to pat a kid on the head and say hello.

One of the most disappointing sights I have ever seen at a cricket ground was at the completion of play in a Test match, one evening outside the dressing room door at the MCG. A lone young boy had been standing, autograph book in hand, waiting patiently some 90 minutes for his hero to emerge.

As most young kids do, the boy had obviously identified with this fast bowler, and used him as a role model — he idolised the man, as I could see by his T shirt, and newspaper clippings in his small hand. The lone boy was told: "Buzz off, kid, I'm busy."

By the time the boy had reached his dad, some 20 metres away, tears of rejection were streaming down his cheeks.

I need say no more. We were all kids once — and how we forget!

Well, I don't forget . . .

It was during the famous 1960-61 Test series between Australia and the West Indies. The touring team was to play a game of cricket in my home town of Hobart, at the T.C.A. ground, elevated high above the beautiful River Derwent.

I was just 11 and I remember the West Indies team were batting against a combined XI.

My burning ambition as a youngster was to play Test cricket for Australia. So I was there in anticipation.

I realised early that day, that the competition for autographs was going to be really tough. In fact, just to get a solitary signature would be a great achievement.

It needed the ingenuity, cunning and guile of a stray dog to succeed.

My ploy was to remove the 10 glass louvre window blades form the toilet area adjacent to the players' dressing room. Gee, I knew it was a gamble, but I thought, "no guts, no glory."

I remember just managing to thread my then-willowy body through the opening in the red brick wall only to land head first on the timber seat of a WC.

Then, one deep breath,with the courage of my convictions,and with blue autograph book held tightly in my hand, I entered the dimly lit West Indies change room!

I was choked with excitement and blushed with embarrassment at just being there.

My hero, fast bowler Wesley Hall, was sitting draped loosely in the corner, against an open locker door.

Lance Gibbs, the Guyanese off spinner was the first to notice me and greeted me with "Where'd you come from, Man?"

After explaining my route into the players' room, via the toilet seat, laughter reigned supreme, and I began to feel much easier.

My request for autographs was immediately granted, without question. I even got two signatures from Big Wes, because my younger sister Lexie wanted the giant fast bowler's scrawl as well.

To this day, I can see their flashing teeth, and huge eyeballs, as they acknowledged my stares.

The images I saw during those precious few minutes are etched in my mind forever.

As you would expect, the stay was short-lived, because Clyde Walcott, (one of the famous 3 W's — Walcott, Worrell and Weekes), the team manager, walked into the room, grabbed me by the scruff of the neck, and drop-kicked me out of the front door of the pavilion!

I am sure the bruise from that size 12 boot lasted on my rear end for about a month — but it was worth it!

Over a decade later, in 1973, as a member of the official Australian cricket team to tour the Caribbean, I again met up with some of my heroes.

Guys like Cammie Smith, Conrad Hunte, Seymour Nurse, Senator Wesley Hall, and — you guessed it — Clyde Walcott!

They were nice enough to say they remembered the incident — but I wonder?

It doesn't matter, because they all played a great part in lighting a fire deep inside me that made me want to be like them. Words cannot express my gratitude.

During the second Test match of that series, in Barbados, I made friends with a young fan named Joey.

It seemed that wherever I was fielding at either end of the ground, Joey would be there on the fence, his face wreathed in smiles, to wish me well. He wasn't brash or cheeky like some other kids, but would greet me with "Gee, I hope you get a wicket this over, Mr Walker," or, after I'd taken one, "That was a great ball, Mr. Walker."

On the final day of the match, spectators as usual invaded the ground, and went through the customary business of crowding the players' balcony, souvenir hunting, and back-slapping.

I noticed young Joey standing there, obviously hoping he would be recognised. I called the little chap over. Somehow he forced his way through the crowd.

Before the game had started, I had been presented with a set of pads and a bat from the Gray Nichols company, which meant that the set of pads I'd had with me since school days were now spare.

When Joey came up to me, I said, "Look if I gave you a pair of pads, do you reckon you could use them?"

I don't think I've ever seen anyone's eyes light up quite so much. " Gee, Mr Walker, we ain't got no pads, we ain't got no bat, we ain't got nothing!"

I gave him the pads, which were almost as big as he was, and off he went, proud as punch into the crowd, with about 40 other kids straggling along behind him.

Strangely, in 1979, I met up with Joey again, during Kerry Packer's World Series Cricket tour of the Caribbean, in which we played five Supertests.

It's hard to believe that the little guy sought me out. By then he was a strapping youth but playing tennis, not cricket.

Maybe I was slightly disappointed, but nevertheless I cherished that young man's friendship, and yet I never knew his last name.

Money can't buy the look on a child's face.

Chapter Four

THE GREAT CHARACTERS I'VE KNOWN

Lillee takes on Javed Miandad. Dennis summed up his attitude: never give a mug an even break.

From Tearaway to Old Ball Master

'I'M SURE SOME OF THEM STILL HAVE NIGHTMARES ABOUT THAT AUSTRALIAN BEAUTY QUEEN'

A bove all else, Dennis Lillee was the complete example of self motivation. Schoolboys roared approvingly . . . male spectators identified with the 'great man' . . . and women loved him!

Statistically he was the greatest bowler in the history of the game (70 Tests, 355 wickets at 23.9).

Dennis summed up his attitude to playing the game he loves in his own words: "Never give a mug an even break!"

During his first class career, which began with Western Australia in the 1969/70 season, he never did give a 'mug' an even break. The only exceptions being when serious injury or illness threatened his career.

It took a near-crippling back injury during the 1973 tour of the West Indies to show the world what a tremendously-determined man he was. That set-back alone would have finished men of lesser talent and, I guess most importantly, of lesser character.

He stayed on during that tour and played as a batsman — yes, a batsman. Although he only played a couple of minor games after the First Test in Jamaica, he wanted to open the batting. It turned out to be a unique experience for Dennis — the young opposing fast bowlers couldn't wait to get at the fastest bowler in the world, with no fear of retaliation.

He copped heaps and couldn't do anything but bite the bullet and face up the next bouncer — just as hundreds of batsmen were to experience against himself in the decade to come.

Lillee's misfortune during that trip was my own good fortune for it enabled me to establish myself in the Australian team under the captaincy of Ian Chappell.

For the next 18 months only Dennis can know of the mental and physical torment he underwent in his endeavors to make a comeback to big cricket. It was during this time that I believe Dennis learned so much of his bowling skills. He played grade cricket for two seasons as a batsman, initially with quite a deal of success too. But as the fractured vertebrae in his lower back healed, the confidence and superb physical condition allowed him to bowl again.

Mostly from a short run and only at slow to medium pace — it was here that he became the master of line and length. Add to this his creative ability to use cut and swing and you have the foundation for a great bowler. He always was the thinking bowler — something different every time.

Lillee came back for the First Test against England in Brisbane 1975. This time he was accompanied by the then new boy Jeff Thomson and myself — it was a terrifying summer for the Englishmen. I'm sure some of

As an opponent they don't come any meaner — he had hate in his eyes.

them still have nightmares about that Australian beauty queen 'Lillian Thomson'.

Dennis had achieved the impossible; Australia had won the Ashes. Lillee again was the idol of Australian crowds.

Many of the characteristics that made 'Fot', as he was known to his team mates, the most recognisable face in Australian sport were emerging: the dark moustache, the hint of larrikinism, the enormous aggression that was to be a feature of his game —both physical and verbal — that gut-wrenching eyeball-splitting appeal and of course the follow through. And no fast bowler in the world has been able to so consistently finish within 18 inches or so of the crease and often eyeball to eyeball with the poor batsman in his follow through than D.K.L. Frightening.

I should know. It was in the summer of 1976 when batting in a Shield game in Perth, Victoria v. Western Australia. I did everything right. I kept my eye on the ball, got in behind the ball, bat, feet and eyes all in a vertical line, but missed the ball travelling at about 95 mph. The first 89 got me, the last 6 mph was a waste of time! And I didn't enjoy the ambulance ride after.

As an opponent they don't come any meaner —he had hate in his eyes. It was a truly intimidating sight to see Dennis turn at the head of his bowling mark and begin to run towards you. To succeed at anything in life you have to 'want it' bad enough — he so desperately did. That is why Dennis Keith Lillee became the greatest fast bowler the world has seen.

The succeeding years weren't always good to Dennis. In 1977 one of the fractures re-opened in the lower back region and he was unable to tour England with the Australian team.

This was another enormous setback considering the Australian summer had concluded with the Centenary Test at the MCG. It could have been his last official Test for Australia.

But Lillee took 11 wickets for the match in an amazing performance of pace, skill and determination. His huge army of fans at the MCG gave him a constant source of inspiration and energy during the five-day encounter —as they have done over a career spanning 15 years.

Looking back over Lillee's career one of the greatest images DKL conjures up in the mind is at the MCG during that magnificent Test match — one that Dennis rates very highly. It is of Lillee turning from the head of his bowling mark and being carried towards the crease in the magnificent free-striding gallop by an enormous crescendo of chanting: "LILLEE! LILLEE!" or "KILL! KILL!"

That love affair with the spectators at the MCG I'm sure is etched in his mind forever — for it was on the same ground several years later that Dennis took his 310th Test wicket to eclipse Lance Gibbs' world Test record.

For two years after 1977 Lillee was a prime mover in the formation of Kerry Packer's World Series Cricket. It began after a conversation with John Cornell over dinner about the amount of payment to cricketers. What happened during the course of the next two years became a part of sporting history and did in fact form an important part of the fabric of first-class cricket in Australia today.

Sure, Kerry Packer and WSC have contributed a lot to cricket, but during the last 15 years no one man has made such a lasting impact on the game internationally as did Dennis Lillee. By the time DKL had bowled his last ball in a Test match, he had made the transition from a 'tearaway' fast bowler to the 'old ball' master. He surely was a master of the fast bowling trade. His subtle variation of pace, angle and length were superb. The leg-cutter was never used more effectively and there was that enormous ability to move the ball either way.

I cannot remember a more devastating five days in Australian sport than that first week in January 1984 at the SCG — Australia v. Pakistan, the fifth Test.

It was marvellous to see Lillee go out in the grand manner we would expect of him, particularly as he had had a disastrous summer in 1984, with a double knee operation to overcome and many, many critics who were calling for his blood.

His own high self-esteem or self-image would not let him quit on a low note — he had to prove to himself and his critics he could still do it. He never doubted he could.

The pity is that by the end of the Australia v. Pakistan series Dennis had made the transition to an 'old ball' master.

He had nevertheless become a very important part of the attack — even though his pace by design was consistently slower, he was still good enough to bowl teams out through his sheer mastery of the fast bowling trade.

His ability to sum up a batsman's weakness quickly and exploit it was second to none. He made physical fitness a new dimension in cricket and finally I must say he was a great psychologist even to the finish.

On Friday, January 6, 1984, Dennis Keith Lillee said goodbye in typical style with a wicket off his last delivery in a Test match. Thanks for the memories, mate! You were the greatest.

Life in the Fast Lane

'HE COULD STIR ALL SORTS OF EMOTIONS, SOME SO PRIMITIVE . . .'

At his peak, Jeffrey Robert Thomson was the fastest bowler I've seen — a magnificent sight from leg gully, but terrifying standing on the batting crease. Ask any English batsman unfortunate enough to have represented his country against Australia in the mid-70s, when Thommo partnered the great Dennis Lillee in one of the most lethal fast bowling combinations to step onto a Test arena.

Together, the pair created havoc against batsmen around the world. During their reign of terror they put the fear of God into even reputable players. Those were the days before World Series Cricket and the development of crash helmets.

David Lloyd, the Lancashire and England opener during the 1974/75 Ashes series in Australia, cautiously faced up to Thommo with a brand new ball. Some say that apart from being frighteningly quick, Thommo's biggest single asset was that he didn't have a clue where the ball was going — so what chance did a batsman have?

Mind you, at speeds in excess of 153 kmh over 22 yards, straight enough was usually good enough . . . it works out that a batsman had something like 0.25 of a second to react to a delivery from Thommo. Not long, eh? And boy can you get hurt if you make the wrong decision . . . forward when you should have gone back.

I'm sure this sort of thought process and self doubt by the short, gritty opener, David Lloyd was the reason why he used to frequently work himself up into such a state that he would actually vomit before he walked to the wicket. It surely wasn't just ordinary nerves getting the better of him — it was terror of Thomson and what he might do.

In fact, I was in Perth during that series and I can vividly recall the Thommo/Lloyd confrontation . . . it was a beauty!

Thommo was really steamed up on the hard, bouncy WACA wicket —the ball kept passing over the top of the stumps after missing the edge. The volatile paceman kept getting more and more frustrated . . . the harder he tried, the faster he bowled. Incredible stuff!

He could stir all sorts of emotions, some of pride, some so primitive they don't make us proud to remember, but that was the perspective of the competitor in Thommo.

His shoulder length mane, flying along behind him as he charged into bowl, the exaggerated side-on turn, the huge athletic kick of the left leg, the right arm coming from behind his buttocks, as he hurled yet another missile at a back-pedalling Pom — it made a team-mate's blood run hot. Not to mention the chanting crowds — they loved him.

Batsmen like Lloyd generally turned a greyish color . . . and with good reason. He unconsciously placed his body, eyes hand and feet in a line behind the direction of the speeding ball, but failed to place the bat correctly. The result was a blow to an area that commentators often describe as the lower abdomen — below the belt buckle, above the pads and between the legs. It was a sickening sound of leather on a plastic protector.

The batsman sunk to his knees, face green and distorted in pain. Huge droplets of perspiration gathered above his eyebrows as he struggled with the agony.

Medical assistance was called for and Bernard Thomas, the England physiotherapist, rushed to his side. Kneeling and hands cupping his face, it was almost as if David Lloyd was deep in prayer.

Australian players gathered round the fallen opponent in token sympathy. Thommo was resting on the ground some 50 metres away, chewing freshly plucked grass from the vicinity of his bowling mark — just waiting to mount another assault.

The damage had been done . . . the seeds of doubt were now well and truly sewn in the mind of the injured man as he was helped from the wicket area.

I guess that's the image many people have of Thommo. The print media made it that way because as the world's fastest bowler he was big news, whatever he did!

Yes, Thommo's name was forever being splashed across the headlines, front and back pages too! Wine, women and wickets; Ferraris, fishing boats and a new dimension to life in the fast bowler's lane.

But to those who played alongside the spearhead, he was mostly quiet, very loyal and fiercely competitive. To Thommo, a mate was a mate, no matter what — the kind of basic spirit of all great sporting teams!

Even a decade after he and Lillee had laid waste to Mike Denness' Englishmen, and Clive Lloyd's West Indians, he was still bowling his heart out for Queensland just as he always did for Australia — like his life depended on it.

Jeff Thomson as I remember him was never a lonely figure but at times enjoyed his own company.

During the Perth test in 74/75 versus England when we were in the field, temperatures had soared in the 40s. We left the ground for tea and a 20-minute rest.

An unthinking official whose sense of timing was terrible, broke the tragic news to the perspiring quickie — one of his closest friends had died after being struck in the chest playing cricket in Queensland. It struck the champion tearaway fast-bowler like a bolt of lightning.

Captain Ian Chappell's ability to read the situation eased the grief. He ordered Thommo to bowl straight away after tea, even though he was in no fit state to do so.

Thommo freely showed his emotions in three very erratic overs through blurry eyes. Chappell had hoped Thommo would vent his rage on the Poms, and that's exactly what transpired! That javelin thrower's action picked up two quick wickets.

Thommo's life was about threatening batsmen with his own lethal philosophy and over the years Thommo and his fellow fast bowlers saw many opposition batters felled.

Sadly, Jeff Thomson bowed out of the game knowing he never played in a successful Sheffield Shield side.

Despite his tough exterior I could sense deep inside he was a shattered man. For the last three summers of his career we saw some Cinderella-like retirements — Lillee, Chappell and Marsh, all retiring on a high note at Test level. Even Clive Lloyd at the SCG in 1985 left with a standing ovation after 110 Tests.

Thommo left cricket like a man leaves an old lover. He just closed the door and walked away for ever. But let's remember he filled summer after endless summer with his brazen fast bowling, his confident, almost arrogant swagger and of course his very quotable quotes. Yes, he always added an extra touch to our game.

So to Jeff Thomson, I say: ashes to ashes, dust to dust, if Lillee don't get you, then Thommo must.

The Greatest Since Bradman

'IT TOOK ME ALMOST 13 YEARS TO RIP HIS MIDDLE AND OFF STUMPS OUT OF THE GROUND'

An Australian batting order without the name Chappell in it seems incomplete! The mere mention of the name instilled confidence in not only the Australian dressing room but also in the majority of people in this cricket-crazy nation. The absence of a Chappell, whether it be Ian, Greg or youngest brother Trevor always left room for doubt.

Both Ian and Greg were given the honour of captaining their country at cricket — probably the highest position in Australian sport!

No other job places so much pressure on the man — both on and off the field of play. Ian was the more successful and acclaimed captain, yet jointly their influence on contemporary Australian cricket has been enormous. Even today when their playing careers are just another set of statistics in Wisden, both men still have a close and important place in the game.

Gregory Stephen Chappell was the second of the three famous cricketing sons. The Chappell family tree links them to their grandfather, the late Victor Richardson.

It was during the fifth Test match in January 1984 between Australia and Pakistan, played at the Sydney Cricket Ground, that Greg pulled stumps on a brilliant Test career. He retired from the international scene just as he entered with a brilliant century (182).

During his final stay at the crease Greg Chappell showed all the qualities that had many experts saying that "he's the best since Bradman". A tag that seemed very appropriate as he overtook Sir Donald Bradman's record aggregate of Test runs (6996) to become the only Australian batsman to score more than 7000 runs in the Test arena.

The innings that day began with the great man showing absolutely no daylight between bat and pad in defence. His backlift was minimal and, as in so many previous innings, his objective of working the ball in only the 'Chappell V' — between mid-on and mid-off — seemed paramount until his half century seemed in reach.

As his confidence grew, so too did the frequency at which he scored. His second 50 was punctuated with several elegant on-drives and square cuts to the boundary. He had achieved his burning ambition to make a century in his goodbye knock. Almost 40,000 light globes burst into a kaleidoscope of colour in the huge electronic scoreboard at the SCG as the entire crowd stood to acknowledge his personal milestone.

He had raised his bat above his head in triumph 24 times before, but somehow on this occasion it was special. Around 19,000 spectators knew they would never see the likes of this man again.

With his score moving beyond three figures, Greg began a cavalcade of scoring shots to all parts of the ground.

It was a beautiful individual expression of the man's superb artistry with the bat — for Chappell was the complete master of his craft and there have been no more pleasing aesthetic sights on a cricket field than Greg Chappell, tall and elegant on the front foot, caressing the ball square of the wicket between point and cover for a boundary.

At times during that memorable final hour at the crease, his attack on the Pakistani bowlers had an air of arrogance — so superior was he.

The images of Greg Chappell are many but he summed up his huge talent in that final innings. His statistical record speaks for itself but it will be the manner and ease in which he collected all of those runs, wickets and catches, that will be etched into the minds of cricket lovers throughout the world.

Had Greg bowled more at Test level I'm sure his return of only 47 Test wickets could have been truly expanded, making him truly one of the world's greatest all-rounders. His 122 catches in Test cricket is also a world record . . . the story goes on.

My memories of Greg are varied — from the 1973 tour of the West Indies where he became the first Australian to exceed 1000 runs on tour. Even then he did it with flair and style. The West Indian crowds under the hot Caribbean sun loved him. "Beat that ball like a bullet out of a gun, man," they would chant as he plundered yet another calypso attack.

He really did bring comfort and pride to his captain and team-mates. With Chappell in the team it just looked a great deal stronger — in this sense he was a terrific team man, if he was in your team!

As a Victorian cricketer I dreaded the thought of playing against him either for South Australia, his home state, or Queensland which is now his home. It took me almost 13 years to rip his middle and off stumps out of the ground!

This memorable feat occurred during the 1981/82 season. I can't say I started the rot but it did see him go through his worst ever run of 'outs'. The champion batsman failed to reach double figures in 14 of his 25 international innings. But to his credit he never doubted his ability as a batsman and showed great character to overcome this bad patch in the face of enormous public criticism.

This was just one of the many times he called on his enormous inner strength. He was not of a physically strong constitution yet his mental toughness was immense — as he again showed during and after the under-arm incident at the MCG, Australia v NZ, 1980/81.

He was booed off the MCG after that little exercise. Two days later he was booed onto the SCG under lights, in the final of the Benson & Hedges WSC. Incredibly, some two hours later he left the field to a standing ovation — such is the man.

The 1977 Centenary Test match at the MCG was one of the many high spots in his brilliant career. Greg captained Australia to a rivetting victory over arch rivals England, to celebrate 100 years of spirited competition between the two countries.

Only 45 runs separated the teams after five days of enthralling cricket — exactly the margin as in their first encounter 100 years earlier. Greg (40) top-scored in the first innings under very difficult conditions — he showed much courage against a fierce English attack on a wet wicket. Remember — and it hurts — Australia only managed 138 in its first innings!

It was individual efforts such as this that enabled Greg Chappell to walk tall in any company. He earned his respect in the middle — not just by talking about it; talk is easy. This enormous respect for the man's ability made him the obvious choice to take over from brother Ian after the 1976 series against the West Indies in Australia.

G.S. Chappell did captain Australia well — he finally achieved a lifetime ambition of leading his country to an Ashes-winning series in Australia during the 1982/83 series.

Ultimately, the enormous media pressure and total commitment to the game, necessary to continue to be successful, forced him to decide between the game he loves, family and business.

The man has a good head on his shoulders — too good to lose to the great game of cricket. He didn't let us down. Today he is a national selector — a job I don't envy him. And one day, Gregory Stephen Chappell will be chairman of the board — the Australian Cricket Board.

A Small Item of Scandal

'EVENTUALLY AN UNDERSTANDING FLOOR MANAGER AGREED'

Some of his mates reckon he does his hair with a rolling pin, but thousands of fans will tell you that Channel Nine's Wide World of Sports co-host Mike Gibson has much more going for him than an undulating head of ginger-blond hair.

'Gibbo' as he is affectionately known to a cult following of lounge lizards on the other side of the silver screen, is really everybody's mate!

He's an earthy character with a relaxed chatty nature. It is easy to relate to the man — he is very much in tune with what the man in the street thinks about sport's controversies.

Gibbo never claims to be an ' expert' yet in many ways he is. As a journalist, and one of the best in Australia, he has a vast track record of following the sport's merry-go-round in many different fields.

And he possesses a mischievous sense of humour as I soon found out.

On a Saturday afternoon the *WWOS* machine is a five-hour epic of live television testing both concentration and intestinal fortitude — we do drink a lot of tea, water and coffee during the program!

After several hours of fluid intake, one's in danger of overflowing, so to speak. The pressure becomes painful, yes, nature must take its course.

I had only been doing the show for about three weeks in Ian Chappell's absence. As subtly as I could suggest, I needed to leave my seat . . . there was a look of shock, horror and disbelief from the producer, so I glanced across at Gibbo. I was hoping he was having a lend of me when he said: "That's just about impossible!"

With two hours of the program remaining I quickly began to go blue in the face. Eventually an understanding floor manager agreed with Gibbo, (who was really enjoying my discomfort) that I really should be released.

I had barely more than four minutes to get back!

Relief, phew . . . there are a very few sensations in the world that can even go close to that one.

I was soon back in the chair smiling like a Cheshire cat and ready to get on with the show.

Then just as I was about to launch into the the next story, Gibbo leaned across to me with his hand over his microphone, and said cheekily, "Maxie, your fly's undone!"

Well, what do you do? It took all my will-power not to look down and I clenched my clipboard tightly to my tie at about naval height.

But sport, and even TV, is a great leveller, and though it was many months later, revenge was sweet.

I arrived at TCN Channel 9 in Sydney early on the Saturday morning to be greeted with a small item of local scandal — Gibbo's cat had a bit of bad luck at his dinner party the night before! Great, I thought, and everyone agreed, that we should mention it on the show — he didn't realise I'd heard about the unfortunate incident.

Then the chance we had all been waiting for . . . we'd just completed a segment on the world equestrian championships.

Now neither Gibbo nor I really know a great deal about equestrian events, so we decided to talk about something other than horses.

"Gibbo, we both love animals a lot, and we talk about them a lot off the air, but is there any truth in the rumour that your cat had a bit of bad luck last night at the dinner party?"

He couldn't believe his ears. How did this scoundrel hear about it? His eyes stood out like golf balls with amazement. Still no comment coming forth.

So I said, "Just a yes or no will do, mate!"

Against his better judgement he finally opened up, "Yeah!"

"Well you can't leave everyone up in the air. Explain what happened!"

So off he went: "Alright, well it was like this — I was carrying the soup bowls back into the kitchen after the first course to put them in the dishwasher! My dishwasher has a lift-down front and a circular shaped window.

"All I could see were these two cat's eyes going around and round in circles!

"My cat must have hopped in earlier in the night to clean off some of the lunch-time plates!"

I asked, "What did you do?"

He replied, "I opened up the front of the washer and out he plonked . . . on the tile floor."

"How was he?" I questioned.

"Oh!" he said, "apart from the two blood-shot eyes, very clean!"

Now there's a message in that story — clean your plates off a little before placing them into the dishwasher, and keep the door shut!

Being Your Country's Keeper

'IT WAS HIS REFLEX ABILITY THAT MADE HIS ONE OF THE MOST SPECTACULAR CATCHES'

The first week in 1984 will long be remembered as the most devastating few days in the history of Australian cricket. It was during the fifth and final Test match between Australia and Pakistan at the Sydney Cricket Ground. In the space of 48 hours, first Greg Chappell, then Dennis Lillee announced their retirement from international cricket.

By the end of that game, Rodney Marsh, the greatest wicket-keeper the world has seen, announced that he would be unavailable to tour the Caribbean at the end of the Australian summer — speculation was rife that this could also mean the end for one of Australia's greatest Test cricketers.

Marsh was to play only the remaining World Series Cup matches, including the three finals, but at the end of the preliminary WSC matches in Perth, on February 4, 1984, he had decided to make the ultimate decision — his time was over! The decision brought to an end the golden era in Australian cricket of the mid-70s when Ian Chappell enjoyed enormous success as captain.

The three-day final series of the World Series Cup saw Rodney Marsh wear the green and gold for the last time, at the MCG — a ground where he shared so many great moments in Australian cricket.

To Rodney Marsh, the 'baggy green' cap, with his country's coat of arms embroidered in gold braid just above the peak, meant everything! He completely identified with the obligations of wearing that cap, and being his country's keeper.

Rod Marsh was never given the opportunity to captain his country in a Test series — one of the few disappointments in his long and distinguished career. There is no doubt, in my mind, that he could have done the job —but he was never invited!

Two brothers, Greg and Ian Chappell, continually consulted the man they used to call 'Iron Gloves', in matters necessary to preserve Australia's high cricket standing in the world. The advice given to the two Australian captains certainly was responsible for many dismissals and ultimately an Australian victory.

Those players, who had shared a dressing room and played alongside Marsh, today rate him as having the best cricket brain playing first class cricket at the time.

My first confrontation with 'Bacchus' was way back in 1967 when Victoria played Western Australia in a Colts match at the MCG. Some other great names to appear in this game were Dennis Lillee (12th man), Bob Massie, Bruce Yardley, Terry Gale (now of golf fame) and for Victoria, John

The man looked sloppy and overweight, but nothing got past him.

Scholes, Alan (Froggy) Thompson and Peter Bedford, who won a Brownlow Medal playing VFL football.

In those days, the man looked sloppy and overweight, but nothing got past him — a feature of his game that was to last right up to the end. Most his career was spent standing back to the faster bowlers. That probably accounts for the fact that he only achieved 12 stumpings from a world record 355 Test dismissals.

Rodney Marsh played more Test matches for Australia than any other man — 96 in all. It seemed a pity that retirement at the peak of his career robbed him of being the first man to play 100 Tests for Australia.

Nevertheless, it should be realised that the solid wicket-keeper with the 'billiard table' legs, also stood behind the stumps in 15 World Series Cricket Super Tests between 1977-79. So, like Lillee, Marsh's official record should be considerably better.

By his own admission, 'Bacchus' has never been a statistics man — great players never are, they let the people tell the story. The cricket-loving public of Australia spent 15 years enjoying the unique entertainment of Rodney Marsh both with the bat and behind the stumps.

I've often heard 'Bacchus' say of a fellow player: "I like the lad, he's got guts!" I will join with many others in saying exactly that about him. Twice he was wounded through the visor of his protective helmet.

No one will ever forget Marsh being felled by a bouncer in Adelaide, during the summer of 1983-84. Azeem, the young Pakistani fast bowler, did the damage — it one of the few times I have seen Marsh leave the field through injury. On this occasion it was with a broken cheek bone and blood-spattered face. A lesser man would not have moved. Yet, only days later against doctors' orders, Rodney was representing his beloved state of Western Australia — and he did it easily.

Rodney Marsh has good hands and I don't mean as a catcher — I'm referring to the continual battering they took over a decade or more, from the fastest bowlers in the world.

During his career I know he has received many letters of caring advice ... some suggesting foam rubber be used, another raw steak instead of inners and even one stated orange skins absorb pain better than anything else.

The man had a fear of X-rays, particularly on his hands, because he believed that if you didn't know they were broken, then they wouldn't hurt as much — a fair philosophy, eh?

Behind the stumps he really was a superb athlete, especially taking into account his build. Remarkably 'Bacchus' took great pride in his ability to defeat many of his 'sleeker' opponents over say, a 40 metre distance.

It was his reflex ability that made him one of the most spectacular catchers the world has ever seen ... he could take the unbelievable. I guess Bevan Congdon, the former New Zealand captain, still wonders how Marsh could have got so far down the leg-side to accept a brilliant catch to a ball that was always going to pitch on the off-stump.

Needless to say the bowler was M.H.N. Walker during the third Test in Auckland. Even to this day, 'Bacchus' rates that as one of his best!

A quite simple way to rate a wicket-keeper is by the number of catches he drops, and believe me, bowlers have long memories in that department — I personally can remember the glove man dropping only one from my bowling in a decade!

I'll bet he remembers it well. It was the first ball of the morning, day two, second Test match, Australia v West Indies at Barbados, 1973. Roy Fredericks on nought went on to make 90-odd. Thanks 'Bacchus'.

I think that it won't be until Rodney Marsh has been out of the game for a while that we will appreciate what a wonderfully consistent and effective keeper Australia had. He didn't let much get past him.

Maybe I've glossed over his career with the bat a little quickly. I apologise, because the same man hit three Test centuries for Australia — no other Australian wicket-keeper had scored one. His last was that memorable 110 not out in the second innings of the Centenary Test against England at the MCG in March, 1977.

After that time Rod's form lapsed, maybe due to the high standard of bowling faced during the World Series Cricket revolution 1977-79.

But not to be outdone, he changed his stance to the new, elevated backlift and the form we used to take for granted returned.

As a bowler ... enough has probably been said, but I know he did enjoy his rare appearance at the bowling crease; so too, did most batsmen.

Rod Marsh was a rebel in his own right. He was his own man, he believed in ability — he did it his way. It wasn't always right, but it was never dull. He played cricket for his country, the way Test cricket ought to be played — fair, uncompromisingly hard and above all — to win.

Maybe that is why young boys the world over identified so readily with the stocky, tough little wicket-keeper from Western Australia. Women adored him ... opposition players knew he meant business when his moustache bristled beneath his cap.

People who know the game appreciate the sportsman in the 'legend'.

He disputed the umpire's decision against Derek Randall in the Centenary Test in Melbourne. Chappell appealled loudly for a caught behind, and was given out. Marsh over-ruled that decision and the batsman was recalled, much to Greg Chappell's dismay.

Randall went on to make 174 runs and almost won that memorable game for England. It has been incidents similar to this one, that have punctuated his career, more often than not going unnoticed.

He has become a father figure to younger Australian players who readily seek out his advice. As 'Bacchus' would say: "They are all Australian and anything I can do to help Australia I will". This is just one more example of his love of his country.

On Sunday evening, February 12, 1984, as Rod Marsh left the MCG for the last time, clad in the familiar green and gold, it was obvious the champion was choked with emotion. He had gone down fighting as always — caught Dujon bowled Garner for 35 — attempting to loft the giant West Indian fast bowler right out of the huge concrete stadium.

At the conclusion of the game, in the Australian dressing room, there was a phone call waiting for him — it was his wife Ros ringing from Perth. "Are you sure you've done the right thing?" she asked.

'Bacchus', we know, said: "Yes" to that question. He always did it his own way and we thank him for his wonderful contribution to Australian sport and I guess we could even say culture!

A swig the skipper didn't see
'THE MAJORITY OF THE MOB BEHIND ME STOOD UP AND CHEERED'

One of my favorite cricket stories occurred during my first tour overseas with the Australian team. That was the 1973 official tour of the Caribbean. Our first stop was Kingston, Jamaica, where we played a handful of games.

As the door of our B.W.I.A. jet opened wide we were greeted with a blast of hot, humid air similar to opening a sauna bath door. Maybe we were lucky because the locals reckoned B.W.I.A. stands for "best wishes if you arrive!" It was worth thinking about though, eh? Some of the small aeroplanes were very old.

I wondered how a bloke like myself could stand up all day and bowl medium-fast anything in this sort of oppressive humidity — believe me it wasn't easy. I thought, gee, I might even hallucinate if I become dehydrated.

It was during this early stage of the trip that I made the decision to make as many friends as I could through the ten feet high barbed wire fences that were obviously built to keep the players inside the playing area for the entire duration of the game! Maybe I could con a drink. It didn't take too long for this theory to prove successful.

The first few wickets that I took whilst in Jamaica were very satisfying but also somewhat unsettling. Every time I returned to my permanent fielding position at deep fine leg I would be greeted with shouts of 'Walker you bad man, Walker!' It was easy to see they weren't smiling when they said that. When they did, and that wasn't often, it looked like piano keyboard set in a large mouth. Too often those smiling mouths were closed ... fortunately things changed as the tour progressed and the calypso singing spectators quickly warmed to Ian Chappell and his Aussies. As one local said, "The cricket's real good man!"

Australia played Jamaica at the Sabina Park Cricket Ground before the first Test match. As usual it had been a very long, hot day and I was approaching my 25th over — I needed a drink, I really did.

My prayers were answered under a cloudless sky that afternoon. The perspiration was leaking from my body like a dripping tap — not one part of my cricket attire was dry. Yes, at last I'd won a friend ... no, not the one that offered me his wife if I took another wicket, but a different guy. He screamed "Wokka, ya wanna drink of my rum.?" It was a deep and bellowing voice. I attempted to explain to him that if the fellow at first slip with the baggy green cap on his head, Ian Chappell, saw me drinking his rum, I would never play cricket for Australia again. His reply was, "Ee won't see ya man!" But 10 foot high barbed wire fences doesn't create a big enough shadow for cover.

With that, the big black man turned to his mate in the back row of the bamboo grandstand. He let out a piercing whistle to catch his friend's attention. Immediately a huge black umbrella was relayed overhead to my new pal in the front row. His name was George.

Before I knew it the umbrella had been thrust through the fence and opened to a diameter of about six foot. I thought to myself, 'There is no way known anyone will be able to spot me having a drink now.'

Through the fence came this dirty, grotty, green bottle of home made rum. I looked carefully at the neck of the bottle — it was not too flash!

Then all the possibilities ran across my mind. I could just have a little sip straight from the bottle — not exactly safe. Maybe if I just dipped my finger in the top of the rum bottle it would be okay. finally I said, "Bugger it, I'll go for the whole catastrophe!" And I did. With the black umbrella for protection, I squatted down on my haunches, and raised the dirty receptacle to my parched lips.

The homemade brew must have been about 500 per cent proof — bloody unreal! I could feel it sting as it passed my cracked lips on its rapid journey to my stomach. It was a strange burning, searing sensation. A 'heart burn' even a Quickeze wouldn't have cured! My Aussie cap almost jumped off the top of my head — this was good stuff, "oh yeah, oh yeah!"

West Indian crowds really react when something tickles their fancy. The majority of the mob behind me stood up and cheered. Some of their very colourful hats and caps were thrown high in the air above their heads. How they got them back, I really don't know.

Now with all this noise, first slip, second slip, cover, mid-off, mid-on and even Rod Marsh the wicketkeeper spun round to see what was happening. I had already handed back 'the brew' to George, who was attempting to dismantle his mate's very large black brolly, but not without a lot of trouble. It was very difficult to tell the difference between some bent umbrella spokes and the barbed wire fence itself.

I just walked away from the crowd as though nothing had happened, although I was coughing from the sting of the rum.

Captain Ian Chappell saw nothing and had nothing to say. I had been successful in partaking of some liquid refreshment and it did the job.

Some two overs later, when I was fielding again in front of my friends in the primitive bamboo stand, things began to happen.

I stood and gazed at that simple structure, which was definitely overloaded by 50 per cent and I thought : 'What chance of this grandstand being designed and built in Melbourne, Victoria? None.

A batsman named Maurice Foster had just hit a lofted pull shot behind square leg. The ball hung in the air for a long time. With all the pace I didn't have, I managed to get close enough to attempt a diving right-handed catch. Without exaggerating, I must have run 40 yards around the boundary line to pull off the catch — it was magnificent. I even rolled over an extra couple of times, after coming to ground heavily, so as to make it look better.

The masses erupted yet again as I came to my feet, brushing the orange dust from my trousers. Every second bloke in the stand swayed to his right as if to mimic the catch. The noise was incredible as my catch was being described over and over again by the cricket enthusiasts. There was no huge electronic scoreboard here to replay the dismissal, only the memory.

I felt obliged to acknowledge the crowd. Obviously it was not my natural pace and ability that enabled me to take the ball safely — it had to be the home-made rum I'd been given! So I began furiously rubbing my hand around in a circular movement over my stomach to show the effects of the jungle juice. Again the crowd roared in acceptance.

At this stage I had my back to the centre wicket area and began really playing up to the colourful spectators. I was enjoying myself when a deathly silence came across the entire ground. I must have been the only person at the ground who didn't realise that it had been called a no-ball and the batsmen had just run three runs. You can imagine the embarrassment I felt, I wish the earth could just swallow me up.

My skipper Chappell didn't take too kindly to this incident, especially as I was a young player on his first tour. Mind you, it didn't exactly cost us the game but I knew then that Ian Chappell was going to be a very firm captain.

He certainly must rate in the best three captains Australia has ever produced, alongside the immortal Sir Donald Bradman and now Channel 9 cricket commentator and journalist Richie Benaud.

It is difficult to discuss the merits of all three gentlemen as Bradman's career finished before I was born. Yet my uncle Charlie, still living in Tasmania reckons 'the Don' was the greatest cricketer — he's probably right. Charlie is the proud owner of a mint-condition record called 'Our Don Bradman' and the 1948 ABC cricket book for the tour of England along with lots of other memorabilia. Herein lies a distinctly biassed yet honest source of my early impressions of the greatest batsman the world has ever seen. The man was a sporting freak.

As a captain, by his own performance with the bat, a century every third innings, he reduced a lot of the burdens experienced when captaining a weaker team not capable of scoring many runs. He led by example and the man's credibility was never doubted — he gained his respect where it counts, in the middle.

Richie Benaud was a childhood hero of mine and along with many of his team-mates he was responsible for setting alight the burning desire inside me to become a Test cricketer. He was one of our great all-rounders and a leg-spinner extraordinaire. Tactically he was very good, as his deeds in the record books suggest. He had that statesmanlike quality that divides the masses from the leaders of men. He still has that quality today when he comments with authority based on a lifetime in the game of cricket.

As I look back on almost a decade of cricket alongside Ian Chappell, I can comment from a first-hand experience on the man, the player and the captain.

So much of Ian's character surfaced in his leadership and attitude to the game. I guess it wouldn't be wrong to say that he was a sort of maverick in Australian cricket. He was super competitive — all the time. The man hated to lose his wicket to anyone because he didn't feel they deserved it. His approach was similar when in control of the nation's best — he never talked of losing, we never talked of losing. Such was the positive direction of the man — he never asked anything more of his team that he wasn't capable of doing himself.

In the field he was extraordinary in communicating with his team. Eyeball contact would be kept up about four times every over with every member of the side. Nobody had to guess what was happening.

Doug Walters, who was splendidly used as a bowler by Chappell knew exactly where he was at. Doug would often be used as the partnership breaker, something he is quite proud of. Usually he would get the unsuspecting batsman to have a fling at a wide delivery outside the off-stump. After the Lillee/Thompson assault this was a picnic but to the unwary . . . danger lurked. Many a catch has gone to mid-off leaving Doug Walters with figures of . . . as Dougie would say, "Bloody beauty one for none!"

Asked what special quality the delivery had, his reply would be, "Width mate, a lesser player wouldn't have got near it!"

Ian Chappell was often pressed to give the boy from Dungog a second over only to be rebuffed with the comment, "Don't push your luck pal, you've already been pretty lucky, now piss off back to slips!" Lillee and Thomson would be brought back into the attack with immediate success . . .

On the question of ACB confrontation he never asked for a show of strength from his players, he just tackled the question on his own and he held himself responsible for the outcome.

To sum him up, he cared only about results and the well-being of his team — he simply cared. He talked to his players, with them, but not often at them. This led to a wonderful team spirit, possibly the biggest single strength his team had during the mid 70's.

Yes, Ian Chappell may just have been the best of those three captains.

Providing the light relief

'SO FROM THE DASHING RIGHT HAND BATSMAN . . . A TRICK FOR ALL OCCASIONS'

While I'm a great believer in not living in the past it's sometimes not a bad idea to share a walk down memory lane when in the company of old friends. That's exactly what I did recently at a sportsnight where the other speaker on the panel was my mate Dougie Walters . . . and boy did we walk down some lanes!

We couldn't help but discuss the successful yet uneasy time we spent in cricket under the captaincy of Ian Chappell. It was during these years between 1972-1976 that we as players were coming under close scrutiny and had been branded as 'boorish' and 'swaggering'.

It was the time of the 'Ugly Australians', a tag given the team after the controversial 1973-74 tour of New Zealand when Chappell clashed with Glenn Turner and the Australian players and the Australian cricket press went to war. The players referred to the writers then as the 'poison typewriter club'.

As usual, it was left to Doug Walters to provide the light relief and, with prank or mimicry, diffuse some of the more tense situations. But he was also a victim on one very significant occasion. It was during the 2nd Test against England at Perth in December, 1974. A confidence trick, at his expense, devised by Ian Chappell and the rest of the team, worked beautifully.

Opening batsman, John Edrich, played one of his very dreary knocks for England, 60 or 70 in about seven hours. Dougie sledged him from go to whoa and declared: "If I'm out there for two hours, I'll get a hundred."

We weren't travelling that well and chasing quite a few. Dougie kept saying: "This is diabolical. We should beat this mob in three days and go fishing." He'd had another big night and there were a few road maps in his eyes. Anyway, came his turn to bat and he was three not out at tea, when he left to go out for the last session, he ordered the room attendant to put champagne on ice.

Dougie batted sensationally and hit the last ball of the day for six to give him 100 in the session. At Chappell's direction, we all went into the showers and toilets so there was no one in the changing rooms when he came in.

He was always on the defensive because he'd served up so much over the years. Eventually Chappell emerged and said: "What are you doing, pal? Don't tell me you're bloody out. We couldn't afford to lose a wicket tonight and you were going so well." Chappelli gave him a real spray and Dougie couldn't work out whether he was serious or not.

101

Dougie stammered: "No Ian, I got a 100 although the board still shows 97. I hit the last ball for a six.

Chappell, struggling to keep a straight face said grimly: "Yeah, that would be right, 97 on the board and you reckon you got 100. And the last ball went for six. You missed the two previous balls by a mile. It was so draughty out there I had to go and get a jumper."

That was too much for Dougie. He poured his guts out and all of us came and gave him a real seeing to. It was one of the few times I've seen him done, and stuck for words.

Doug Walters always made a point of knowing each player's pet aversion. In the case of lanky off-spinner 'Rowdy' Mallett it was spiders.

In fact it was at the MCG in the same series that Ashley Mallett the off-spinner suffered because he had showed little respect for his team-mates when it came to handing out and sharing the team's chewing gum.

For the first two days Mallett would grab every piece of chewing gum left on the rub-down table in the small white saucer. Before play, before the middle session of play, after lunch and after the tea break, his penchant for gum would get the better of him. This was all too selfish, thought Dougie! The devious mind began to work overtime.

It must be mentioned that 'Dungog' Dougie has been inside almost every trick shop in the world and what's more he has usually made a purchase while there! So from the dashing right hand batsman . . . a trick for all occasions.

The scene was set immediately after we had all eaten lunch on the third day's play.

Boot laces were tied, shirts tucked in and suntan lotion freely applied to sunburnt faces. The unsuspecting Mallett knocked over three of his team-mates getting to the package with just a solitary stick of gum remaining.

Now to get out of the dressing room at the MCG, the players have to climb a 16-step carpeted staircase with a landing halfway up. By the time the clumsy off-spinner had reached the landing, he'd unwrapped the package to get to the stick of gum.

Well, out of the package sprang the biggest black rubber tarantula you've ever seen . . . it was still wobbling when it hit the floor. A terrified Mallett lived up to his reputation of being a little clumsy because he pushed his hand down to break his fall and crunch — the three sprigs of the heel of of his left boot punctured the back of his bowling hand. Three tiny bubbles of blood appeared on the back of his hand, getting bigger by the second!

After everyone had a great laugh, 'Rowdy' received the necessary medical attention and appeared on the hallowed MCG turf sporting a cross made up of two Bandaids.

When Dougie and I finally stopped exchanging our own experiences that night on the panel, the focus turned to other characters and other tours. With the state of world politics today being forever married to sport, we could not help but touch on the subject of South Africa. Doug had toured there with the last official Test team in 1970 and I was fortunate enough to get an invite with Richie Benaud's International Wanderers side in 1976.

This tour provided me with one of the most stirring experiences of my career. The Wanderers, with John Shepherd, the Barbadian, the only coloured player in our ranks, played a match against an all black XI in the appalling city of Soweto, south-west of Johannesburg. Our team members were the only whites allowed in the ghetto that day.

Johnny Shepherd's company was an absolute joy. Blessed with a sharp wit and engaging smile, Shepherd was an itinerant cricketer, and at one time played grade cricket for Footscray in Melbourne.

He played only five Tests for the West Indies and was effectively ostracised by the Caribbean authorities when he played Currie Cup for Rhodesia in 1975-76. A man of immense character and courage, he steadfastly refused to believe his colour should bar him from playing cricket anywhere.

Sitting in a bus one day I remember he said: "Maxie, don't you worry. One day we blacks are going to take this country right over. But don't you worry pal, I'll be Minister for Youth, Sport and Recreation, and I'll get you a job in the garden."

When we got to Port Elizabeth, he headed for the changing-room for the blacks, while the rest of the team headed for the white change rooms. I didn't care about all that rubbish, so I went along with 'Shep'. The room was pokey, to say the least. The whites had a vast area, one room leading off another and then another.

As we were getting changed, I looked across at 'Shep'. He'd got talcum powder under his arms, was awash in after shave and he was going for the sunburn cream. I couldn't believe my eyes! He's got to be the best-smelling cricketer I've ever encountered. His kit bag had everything from Bandaids and linament to exotic perfumes. It was incredible.

'Shep' was not half past eleven, he is really midnight and I had to ask why he was putting on the sunburn cream. "You've got to be joking man. That's not sunburn cream, that's just leather conditioner, that is!"

I enjoyed his company socially and knew he deserved his exceptional popularity throughout South Africa. Among other things, Shep was an excellent communicator between black and white factions and a wonderful asset to have on tour.

It was Shepherd who brought the two teams together after the match at Soweto for a social exchange of ideas and talk about the game.

But most of all, Shepherd was my sort of character because of his great sense of humour and fun. He would laugh at the idiosyncracies of the whites and would laugh at being black in a white society. He was a cricketer who liked to laugh a lot.

Epitome of the English Lion

'HE IS SUPPOSED TO HAVE CAROUSED FOR NIGHTS ON END'

Ian Terence Botham's magnificent career statistics in runs and wickets will assure the British Blockbuster a place in cricket history. It has been a remarkable journey for the great all rounder — a career marked by glorious deeds on the field and marred by considerable turbulence off it.

Yet the numerical aspects of cricket do not consume Botham as they did Geoff Boycott during his long innings in the game.

This colourful character has no idea of how to go about playing for a not-out. When he walks to the crease to bowl, maiden overs have never had much appeal for him, especially if he can take wickets while conceding runs.

Botham epitomises the symbol of English cricket — the lion — even to the way he wears his mane of hair.

His clash with cricket administration in early 1986 was caused by loyalty to his longtime West Indian friends and Somerset team-mates Viv Richards and Joel Garner. They were sacked by his county team Somerset when Martin Crowe, the elegant young New Zealander, was given an overseas players contract.

Botham said he would not play with Somerset the next season. It is typical of the hard-hitting, hard-headed cricket hero.

Barely a day goes by that the burly mega star doesn't have his name set in bold block letters on the front or back pages of a newspaper.

Unfortunately 'Both' is a Pom and Britain's media is notorious for focusing a relentless spotlight on the behavior of the country's sporting heroes. Every day he pays heavily for what the Fleet Street boys see as his excesses away from the cricket pitch.

I'm certain if he was an Australian he would be allowed a lot more latitude, simply because he's a bit of a larrikin and above all else, he knows how to play cricket. My feelings are that Australian cricket writers tend to ignore a player's escapades and extra-curricular activities provided he doesn't run on the wrong side of the law!

It will be fascinating to see if he can rise above all the personal pressures that are bound to follow him as he settles in Australia. His record as a 'survivor' must at least give him a fair chance of coming out on top. I'll be surprised if he doesn't.

I first played against Ian Botham in 1977 — he was a raw, young talent in those days. The youngster had spent some time earlier in his career in Australia on a Whitbread scholarship. He played his Australian cricket with Melbourne University without any significant success.

Yet he must have benefited from the Aussie experience and the good coaching he received from the Lord's ground staff formed a foundation on which to build his game.

Images of Botham playing cricket are forever etched into my mind, much in the same way a sports photographer would set out to capture a game . . . they only look for the highlights or the unusual, and Botham fits both these categories.

Botham would only need to spend 20 minutes at the crease for any cricket photographer worth his salt to get a dozen or so good shots, whereas a two-hour session endured with a Geoffrey Boycott would be lucky to yield a couple of images — the forward defence and letting the ball go!

In many ways Ian Botham is like Dougie Walters . . . they both have the ability to forget about yesterday's failure. They just focus their attention on the job at hand.

Asked a while back why he didn't swing the ball that much anymore when he bowled, Botham replied: "Because they're making the balls differently these days."

Well, he may be partly right, but I'm sure a lighter, fitter Ian Botham who practised hard and regularly, could get it back — discipline in that area of practice is something that neither 'Both' or Dougie could warm to!

From all reports, Ian Botham is a complex man forever seeking the solitude of a fishing trip or a walk for charity . . . yet at the same time needing space to party on with friends like Mick Jagger or Elton John.

Given the choice of an even of analytical discussion with a former great or the opportunity to sink a few ales with the boys at the local pub — he'd invariably choose the latter.

Botham cares little about pride of performance every time he walks on a cricket field, so little in fact that any club hacker could be giving him a frightful thrashing in a benefit match and he would never be stirred to lift his game. I know for a fact that someone like Ian or Greg Chappell or Dennis Lillee wouldn't shrug off the situation with, "Who gives a stuff, it's only a social match!"

Botham's amazing constitution and cricketing ability were never more evident than in the Jubilee Test against India at Bombay in the late '70s, when he scored a century and took 11 wickets in the match. He is supposed to have caroused for nights on end, at one stage going sleepless for three nights.

Keith Miller, the great Australian all rounder of the '50s, is legendary for those sorts of performances . . . maybe it comes with the territory?

While the Bombay Botham performance is not generally known to the public, it has become part of Test cricketers' folklore.

In recent times I have watched with interest the career of I.T. Botham and the awesome features with bat and ball now do not appear to give him the same satisfaction.

During Australia's last Ashes tour in England, it was my privilege to see

105

Images of Botham playing cricket are forever etched into my mind.

Drinks were spilt in an effort to get a glimpse of the dasher.

Alan Border score a great century at Lord's to win our only Test match for the series. I led and enthusiastic tour group.

It was fascinating to observe the old codgers in the Long Room in the historic members stand — it is through this room that the Test players must pass on their walk to the wicket. I'm sure Ian Botham has mixed thoughts about these incredibly stuffy 'gentlemen' who occupy English cricket's most sacred room on Test match days.

Normally they sit there sporting bristling handle bar moustaches, their pin-stripe suits showing their affluence . . . yet batsmen like Geoff Boycott or Chris Tavare bore them.

Usually the front two rows of seats are punctuated with sleeping Wing Commanders and titled Tories. But let the charismatic figure of Botham appear in the great spaces on his way to bat, and drinks were spilt in an effort to get a glimpse of the dasher.

Chapter Five

AS I ALWAYS SAY . . .NO GUTS, NO GLORY

The horse's head dipped as I slid up the main.

Leave it to the little blokes
'EVEN THOUGH HE HAD EYE FLAPS ON, I COULD SEE HIM LOOKING AT ME'

From time to time sportsmen get asked to be involved in some pretty crazy fund raising exercises and generally I think their contribution to the various charities is fantastic. But there are occasionally situations which eventuate that really should have been thought over a lot more before saying "Yes!"

At 6'4" tall and conservatively, a big-boned fella, I'm not your average jockey! In fact I've had no aspirations to being a jockey — yet it happened.

Raelene Boyle, the golden girl of athletics, actor Tony Bonner and myself were invited to compete in a celebrity trotting event at the Moonee Valley Racecourse in 1985.

Now, to ride or drive a sulky a lap or two of this great racecourse, that really is something else.

The last time I can remember having a ride on a horse, was as a 14-year-old pimple-faced schoolboy in Hobart.

At the time I was tracking square, with a fresh-faced 12-year-old farm girl from just out of town. She even organised for me to have a bit of a gallop on an old grey mare, "gentle soul" she said, but that was only until my friend slapped the huge dotted mare on its hind quarters.

When you're sitting high above the ground on a runaway 'neddy', you really get an appreciation of pace. My mount pulled up after several minutes of frantic galloping —headlong at a rusty old fence. The horse's head dipped and I slid straight up the mane until I grabbed hold of the animal's ears. It was a temporary halt only, because I ended up on the other side of the wire fence, much to the laughter of my sweet young maiden.

We didn't remain friends for much longer — she had a different sense of humour to me. And she also loved horses, I definitely didn't!

I had almost forgotten the incident until the practice run at Moonee Valley. Some practice run!

I guess Raelene has always been a pacer and she took it all in her stride. They tell me horses love the soft touch of a woman. That fact alone didn't help my chances, a big gorilla like me.

Tony Bonner was great. He raced several times around the track as though he'd been a trotting driver all his life — he's probably played the role of a cowboy a few times as well, eh?

Then it was my turn. I smiled through clenched teeth but I didn't feel at all confident. My horse was a beautiful chestnut stallion, a magnificent creature. Even though he had eye flaps on, I could see him looking at me. I knew he wasn't impressed! Why should he be! I weighed in excess of 100 kilos.

As I buckled up my shiny blue helmet, the horse's strapper Cheree was patting the horse's neck to console him. It was a cold morning and the horse's breath came from its flared nostrils like discharge from an exhaust pipe — maybe that was significant. Gee, I was hoping the horse and I could be friends.

My next task was to get myself seated on the apparatus — I think they called it a sulky. Two wheels, a fixing rail and just a few square inches of seat on which to fix the muscles of one's bottom and then hang on tight. At this stage my knees were up around my throat, so short was the previous reinsman's legs.

Just a couple more explanations and I would be away . . . or that's what I thought. With the reins held fairly tightly I was told, "pull the left rein once to turn left; pull the right rein once to turn right; pull them back solidly towards yourself to stop. And of course to take off . . . just a slight flicking action will be sufficient."

Maybe I flicked too hard, because this huge horse reared straight up. The cheeks of my bum tightened as I felt myself sliding backwards. I was now hanging on for dear life with the reins wrapped tightly around each hand. I was probably pulling too hard and hurting the horse's back teeth, but then the buggy was standing at about 70 degrees to the ground — and I must say it was not easy to maintain my cool.

Finally some order was restored and we somehow got the stallion's two front feet back on the ground. Whew! What a pleasing sight.

Everyone else, including the strapper, was doubled up laughing at me.

Cheree suggested we just walk one quiet lap with her sitting side saddle beside me. I agreed. At least it was a start. It seemed like eternity to complete just one circumference at Moonee Valley.

"Now," she said, "Maxie, it's your turn, just trot him gently around the track!"

"Gently!" I replied. "How do I get him to walk gently for me — he hates me!"

Nevertheless we took off ever so slowly, horse and strapper side by side and yours truly being dragged along at the rear. We were really looking good until the pace, like my heartbeat, quickened. Although it was only a trot from here on in it was also a frightened man.

Things went along nicely until about a quarter of a lap further on, one of the local trotting drivers was putting his trotter through its paces on the inside. He was really flying — a beautiful black stallion in full flight.

I guess the competitive spirit in my horse quickly surfaced at the sight of another trotter running so fast. My horse just laid back his ears, put his head down, snorted loudly from his nostrils and took off towards the inside running rail in hot pursuit.

I just hung on — it was frightening stuff watching the ground pass so quickly beneath my seat. The shell grit from the flailing hooves in front kept on striking my contorted face, forcing me to squint. I'd forgotten the goggles.

110

Quite incredibly we apeared to be making ground on the big black fella in front . . . then all the negative thoughts kept sapping my enjoyment. What if I fall off now — good luck! I don't think my insurance policy will cover this one. Gee, I hope they haven't got a camera on me now . . . and so on.

In no time at all the lap was completed and I did what I was told. I pulled the long leather straps, to stop at where I began the ride. My horse didn't like it. We ended up coming to a halt some 100 metres past the rest of the gang. Again they thought it all a great joke.

After my rescue, caked in shell grit and much, I suggested there was no way known that I would ever get on a horse again. Especially not alongside five or six other untrained trotting drivers of dubious sporting background. No way! Never.

All I wanted to do was have a shower and get out of the place. So we ventured into the holy of holies at Moonee Valley Racetrack (the jockeys' changing room) — a special privilege to get in here.

I can understanding why — the place is designed purely for jockeys. Talk about low slung showers, it was impossible to get anything above my navel wet. All the shower heads were set on the wall at 4'6". I ended up sitting on the cold mosaic tile floor in order to get my hair wet. I was a bit worried about getting haemorrhoids!

Having towelled myself down with a towel more like a handkerchief, I spotted some scales in the corner. Weight is pretty important to a jockey — not so important to a footballer or a cricketer. You won't believe this. The scales only went up to 10 stone in imperial measure. That left me well short of the mark and unsure as to whether or not I'd lost any weight during the event.

Even to sit on a chair to do my boots up was uncomfortable. It was just like sitting on the floor. Yes, it really is another world. I admire the courage of those fellas when they climb up on to a horse for a big race. Once was enough for me.

The one that got away
'THE FINE NYLON CORD CUT LIKE A KNIFE THROUGH MY INDEX FINGER'

The 55 kg breaking strain nylon fishing line snapped as the tiny loop around the shiny metal bollard fastened tightly. Whatever had momentarily caught on the other end of my rapidly diminishing handline, treated the fine, almost invisible thread, like a piece of cotton!

It was difficult for a relatively non sea-loving person like myself to gauge the power and dimensions of the creature lurking beneath these sparkling blue-green tropical waters. Not to mention the danger!

The action of my leather-gloved companion in yanking against the pull of the rapidly disappearing nylon tackle, then gaining sufficient slack to wrap it once around the chrome-plated bollard which was fixed to the boat's handrail, certainly saved me getting wet, maybe even losing the bottom half of my right leg. True to form I had tangled most of the line in a mess beneath my feet. No wonder my nickname's Tanglefoot!

I began pulling in what I thought was about 3 or 4 kilos of fish, but some monster of a fish had other ideas and must have followed my catch on its painful journey to the surface.

Then, without warning, my hand-line whistled through my helpless fingers at a frantic pace, back into the depths below. the fine nylon cord cut like a knife through the index finger of my right hand. Blood streamed freely from the tiny crack . . . a burning sensation followed and I immediately let go of the line. What had I snared on my line?

My bare feet thrashed up and down like a piston in an attempt to keep clear of the snaking fishing line as it disappeared over the edge.

Directions were being shouted at me from everyone, but too late. I was desperately in trouble with my footwork — the fine, pale green fishing line was pulling taut against my right leg, just above the ankle . . . three or more coils tightened. Blood dribbled slowly down my leg . . .

But worse was that I was being dragged overboard by the leg! Yes, the huge fish was winning this tug of war and I couldn't get my hand near the razor sharp line! Not that it would have done much good without a glove!

My host, Gary realised the seriousness of my predicament before my head crashed against the aluminium bottom of the twin-hulled Shark Cat. What a sight — my legs pointed unwillingly to the clear blue sky!

His experience quicky showed as he grabbed my line . . . the rest is history. A classic case of the one that got away. He would have been a beauty! But . . . just as well that line snapped, eh?

It was purely a laughing matter for my mate, Dougie Walters, but I shudder to think what might have happened had I splashed overboard and into the ocean.

Mind you, there was no shortage of sarcastic suggestions for about 15 minutes . . . "See, Tangles you could have ended up like that guy who tried to harpoon Moby Dick and you didn't even throw a dart . . .!" or "Gee, Tang you might have drowned.

My mates on board continued to take the mickey out of my painful, unfortunate incident, as I patched up my wounds. A band aid sufficed on my index finger but my pure white leg looked like a pillar from outside an old fashioned barber's shop. And the salt water in my cuts didn't help much either.

The accident taught me a couple of hard lessons.

Firstly, never wear thongs in a boat while you're fishing, and definitely don't wrap the hand-line around your fingers when fishing in deep waters — you may lose 'em! Still one learns by experience. But what an experience — and it didn't stop there!

The secret location where our guides stopped to wet the lines, was called 'The Chasm' — about an hour off the coast of Groote Eylandt in the Gulf of Carpentaria, east of Darwin.

We were taken to the spot by two off-duty Northern Territory policemen, who turned out to be magnificent hosts. They also mentioned to us that it would be just a matter of dropping down anchor, and the fish would literally jump into the boat . . . and strangely it turned out to be exactly that way, except in my case, I almost ended up in the drink!

Everything was just beginning to quieten down again . . . including the mocking laughter, when I was asked to have a look over the side of the boat, opposite to where I was fishing. It was still only 7 a.m. with the sun barely in the sky.

I could see by the expression on Dougie's face I really ought to take a peep! No cheeky grin, his eyes narrowed and what little colour he had in his cheeks disappeared. It was the biggest fish I've ever seen!! There it was, a huge, charcoal grey shadow gently nudging our craft, only an arm's length away from where I stood, speechless.

I could tell it was a shark because I'd sat through Jaws 1, 2 and 3 with extreme discomfort. And I know a shark fin when I see one.

This fella must have been almost eight metres long . . . like a baby submarine. One of the policemen suggest we shoot it . . . in fact he even took aim with his hand gun.

But judging by its size anyway, I'm sure the bullet would have just ricocheted off the shark's sinister skin — this may have been the beauty I missed, and just as well too! Because with him on tow I know who would be taking who for a ride.

Once my blood started flowing and the shark left the scene, we got on with the job of serious fishing.

In all, our catch consisted of a variety fo fish — about 55 of 'em! And as predicted it had been just a matter of putting bait on the hook and dropping it in the ocean. I soon regained my confidence to land a 20 kilo Jew Fish . . . Dougie's best effort was a feeble 3 or 4 kilo job.

All this happened after I'd just completed reading the script for a new television commercial . . . yours truly was cast in the role, unfairly, as the world's worst fisherman.

Who do you think my partner in the dinghy is? My mate and former cricketing great Dougie Walters.

I suppose he'll catch a whale and I'll hook a sardine . . . only time will tell. But one thing's for sure we were both going to get very wet in the process.

Let's hope there's no sharks around and the water is warm . . . given the option of four glittering hamstrings dangling in the water. The betting is that any hungry 'Noah's ark' would head for my pure white Melbourne ones with their moonlight tan!

The odds on the average racegoer becoming wealthy after a day at the track are pretty remote.

A mug punter out in the cold
'HE WASN'T TOO IMPRESSED WITH MY SHIRT'

How many times has a friend or workmate offered to let you share a hot tip at the races with words like, "You've gotta back so and so in the fifth . . . it can't lose!"?

In good faith you hand over your hard earned cash . . . maybe $20. Well, that's about my style because I'll be honest, I barely know which end of a horse to feed.

Strangely enough, I've never yet collected over more than a decade of accepting inside knowledge, with a view to getting rich quick. Because the odds on the average racegoer becoming wealthy after a day at the track are pretty remote.

So with this fact at the backs of their creative minds, Toohey's advertising agency, Mojo, came up with a script for a 30-second TV commercial that placed Dougie Walters and myself right in the middle of all those hay burners.

Now Dougie has been known to have both a bet and a beer in the past, so the former champion cricketer slipped into the role of rogue punter as easily as pulling on a batting glove.

As for myself . . . well, I've never even been to the Melbourne Cup. Anyway it seemed like a good plot.

The small farming township of Quirindi was the chosen location — about half an hour's flight out of Sydney airport.

Dougie thought he ought to travel to the location by car with 'China' from Kersey Films, the production house. They planned on arriving the night before the shooting of the commercial . . . so as to get in a little practice for the beer tasting that obviously would take place on the set.

Everything seemed rosey for the two lads as they cruised along the highway in their late model Ford Fairlane. They weren't to know what lay ahead.

The customary stop for petrol proved catastrophic for the thirsty duo. After almost 70 litre of fuel had been emptied into the petrol tank, the ever watchful eye of Dougie, the passenger, turned to check out the cost rotating on the face of the bowser . . . maybe he'd have to pay half?

Shock! Horror! are hardly the words used to describe what the would-be TV punter discovered . . . the tank was almost totally full of diesel, not leaded petrol as expected. Any attempt to move the car produced a pitch black smoke screen.

Our all-Australian hero and veteran of two years' national service called on his experience behind the wheel of the odd diesel truck . . . "We'll have to get the diesel completely out of the system!" was the authoritative observation.

115

It was a bit early in the day for a 'red wine' but 77 litres of diesel fuel had to be siphoned out of the petrol tank through a very narrow plastic tube. Needless to say a certain quantity of the intoxicating liquid had to be swallowed in order to get the siphon working . . . even a Tooheys 2.2 couldn't make the unpalatable taste disappear.

So for his efforts of sucking diesel through a narrow gutted flexible hose, 'China' was soon to be nicknamed 'Syphon', which he didn't really like.

Two hours later the safari to the picturesque Quirindi Racetrack got back on the road . . . with an irritating ping in the motor and a tell-tale cloud of dirty black smoke spewing out of the exhaust pipe.

Exceeding the speed limit was the last thing the luckless pair had on their minds — the big question was would the noisy Fairlane go the distance without another hold-up?

Then came the blue flashing light, and the inevitable, "Pull over driver!"

A rather colourful explanation of the chain of events over two cigarettes by Dougie almost got the duo a police escort . . . similar to those given pregnant ladies on the way to the maternity hospital.

Without further incident the dry-humored man from Dungog and his distraught driver arrived in town . . . "We'd better have one before we check the track," was not an unexpected suggestion from Dougie.

It was in the bar of the Commercial Hotel that the travel-weary pair shared a beer with Stanley, a 60-year-old bitzer who reckoned he had Indian, English and Aboriginal blood in his veins. Stanley worked with Johnny at the racetrack (whoever Johnny was), but in most country towns everyone knows everyone.

Now Doug's reputation as a cricketer and all-round good guy had preceded him and the locals were very much looking forward to the two days' filming.

Before they left the watering hole that afternoon, Stanley left the pair with some words of wisdom about two types of blokes you should never employ. "Never employ a smoker who spends $2 an hour rolling smokes, and never employ a man who wears a straw hat on windy days!"

Another early arrival at Quirindi was Rocky a camel. This fellow and owner arrived about a week early because the horses needed to get used to the camel, if that is possible. Horses are terrified of camels. Several stable doors were kicked down by frightened horses during Rocky's stay!

Anyway to the big day. The usual preliminaries of selecting which wardrobe to wear and of course how can we forget the make-up?

Two hundred or more of the townsfolk turned out to enjoy a free champagne and chicken breakfast — compliments of Tooheys.

The event brought a mixed reaction. The local newspaper, the Quirindi *Advocate,* published many letters expressing their point of view.

A front page headline read: HORSES DON'T DRINK BEER!

Despite some negative vibes, the crowd had assembled on the grass outside the grandstand and the setting was perfect, apart from the temperature of 8 degrees Celsius.

I don't have to tell you but we both looked the part . . . a couple of out-of-town punters just up for the day's racing — complete with hats and Members' enclosure medallions.

The gist of the story is that Doug knows everything about racing and has the good money placed. As for yours truly, well I am a bad punter out of luck. The bookmakers, with names like Col Slaw and Paddy Field saw me coming.

Before long I've lost every penny I own on these hopeless chaff-eaters . . . and even the shirt off my back which I offer to the bagman in question — a big rubber-faced bloke called Neville. How could I ever forget him?

He wasn't too impressed with my shirt with the inference that I had an underarm problem — wasn't that Trevor Chappell?

At this stage my mate Dougie can see I'm in trouble and pulls up with a rack full of shirts. I'm freezing cold standing in my cotton singlet, with a tie draped around my bare neck, thinking about what might have been.

With tongue in cheek Doug offers me the first shirt on the rack — I check it for quality and the little fella lays this line on me: "A bit of fine cotton here Tangles!"

I sarcastically usher him away.

The next shot is much better — I can put my coat on plus the garish blue shirt that Doug has selected for me!

Dougie and yours truly — a couple of out-of-town punters up for the day's racing.

Seated at a table, elevated on another table to suit the director, Bob Kersey — a brilliant man who knows exactly what he wants and gets it — we are perusing the form guide with a couple of 'frosty heroes', or cans of Tooheys 2.2, never more than an arm's length away.

My line is something like "I wouldn't know the difference between a stayer and a schooner."

A sneering slit-eyed acknowledgement greets my comment.

The well dressed punter on my right then asks if I've got a tip in the last. I've got no money but I'm pretty happy to recommend No. 6.

As the camera focuses on the barrier — number 6 turns out to be Rocky the camel. Needless to say Doug didn't take any notice of my tip in the last and backed his own.

All in all it was a marvellous couple of days and I trust the finished product was as good as the previous three commercials — golf, fishing and darts.

White man down a hole

'I REACHED THE SAFETY OF A FARAWAY TUNNEL WITH 73 SECONDS TO SPARE'

I've played cricket in almost every cricketing country in the world. Some of the Test match venues have had a beautiful lush green covering of turf, combed in a geometric pattern parallel to the equally well prepared centre wicket area, such as at Lord's in England.

Other grounds such as Port of Spain in Trinidad used to make diving in the outfield feel a bit like diving on razor blades — the wicket itself was not unlike grade nine sand paper, a very abrasive surface indeed.

But never have I seen anything quite like the football-cum-cricket ground at Coober Pedy.

It even has a racetrack around the perimeter if you could call it that! I'm sure the scant metal pipe fencing is only to stop the cheeky little jockeys from taking a short cut across the playing area. Many people have said to me, "It's different in the centre," and they're not wrong. Wonderfully different!

For many years I had been very keen to travel to the centre of this great country of ours. I've seen too many first class hotels and major cricket grounds in Australia's populated cities around the coastline. "What is the real Australia like?" That's the question a 'little fella' inside of me has been continually asking.

Well, now I know first hand and believe me I'm not disappointed. Incredible!

It has been said that the only way to achieve anything in life is to make it happen yourself. Well, make it happen I did. With the help of my good friend

Graham Charlton from radio station 5RM Berri in South Australia, a speaking engagement was arranged for me in Coober Pedy.

Coober Pedy is an Aboriginal name for 'white man in a hole'. It seemed a fairly apt description after seeing some of the dwellings of the residents.

Driving from Adelaide, as we approached this unique town, the horizon appeared much like a purple moonscape. The setting sun brought down the curtain on a fabulous day, rich in red dust and briliant blue skies. Everywhere we looked were huge ant-hills or mullock heaps — riles of waste rock and earth collected neatly on the barren surface.

My reason for being there was to entertain the locals at a sportsman's night. I wondered how many people would turn up to see me perform at the Opal Inn. In fact how many of the townspeople even knew who Max Walker was?

The answer could not have been more pleasant — especially as it was a Saturday night and we were competing with the re-opening of Porky's night club just down the road.

The night was mixed for gals and guys — standing room only. There was of course the odd rowdy element and local comedian in the audience but it all added to a very good night. The hospitality of the community was as good as I've ever received.

I was standing at the bar when Terry and Peter made themselves known . . . I'm not sure but it must have been well after midnight.

They were a couple of genuine guys, opal miners, who, by the way, had already had a very good night. It seemed crazy at this hour that we were making serious plans to go below the earth's surface at 7 o'clock in the morning in search of that rare and wondrous gem — the opal.

I thought: why not — you're dead a long time, and I'll never get another opportunity to mine opal. Just the thought of it made the adrenalin pump a little faster. But I didn't know what to expect.

Nevertheless shortly before 8 a.m. I found myself sitting on a piece of scantling timber about 50 x 25 mm in section, fitted crudely to a steel wire pulley system to form a lowering apparatus. That was to be my ride down into the depths of the mine — a bit hard on the bum too that early in the morning. But with a nickname like "Tanglefoot", worse was to come.

I had to fit down a one metre wide access shaft which was about 20 metres deep. My two mates had disappeared below the surface with just the steel cable for support and a plastic stack hat on their heads in case a rock fell down on top of them — nice thought, and very possible too!

Only a corrugated iron tank, with the top and bottom missing, prevented the surface edge of the hole caving in. A very flimsy looking rusty ladder hung from a casually resting 50 mm steel pipe on one side of the small opening, just in case any trouble was encountered.

My first problem was the length of my leg from the seat of my pants to the point of my knee cap. At one stage it looked as if I might have to go down standing up and not sitting down —what was I doing here?

Well I did make it to the bottom but not without collecting every second rung of that metal ladder with my awkwardly folded knees as I rotated anti-clockwise to the bottom. Talk about housemaid's knee — both of mine felt like they had enormous church bells ringing inside them. I suppose being that far underground my pain barrier ought to be pretty low too.

Surprisingly the space below was like a well defined cave with drives or tunnels shooting off it in seven or eight directions.

We were told that geologically Australia is the world's oldest land, with some of its rock being formed as long ago as three billion years, and that 95 per cent of the world's opals are mined in Australia.

Millions of years ago non-crystalline silica gel seeped into crevices and cracks in the sedimentary strata. Gradually over eons, the gel hardened, capturing within it darting, glowing colours that dance and leap as different angles of light bring them to the surface. Opals have a life and inner fire all of their own.

Black opal is the most sought-after, in fact more valuable than diamonds. It is rare and considered to be the ultimate in gem beauty — a bit like holding a little bit of outer space in your hand — filled with stars of brilliant colors.

Time was the essence, and it didn't take the bearded Peter long to get down to business. He quickly set about making up nine explosives. To him it was like making up a paper bag full of lollies. I said, "What happens if one of those things goes off?" His reply was simple: "I wouldn't worry too much — if it does go up you're not going to know much about it anyway!" A nice comforting thought, eh?

Each of the long slender brown paper bags, approximately 50 mm in diameter, was gently filled with tiny grains of Nitro-Pril — I didn't bother to ask Peter what Nitro-Pil was but I had a fair idea! One by one they were placed almost lovingly on the rough textured sandstone floor.

Idle, nervous chatter continued until all the explosives were knotted and positioned inside the sinister little bags. When all nine were completed, wicks intact, the tiny, lethal detonators were taped to each stick — just like in the movies!

Now the morning was beginning to get interesting. I quickly scraped the sleep and dust from the corner of each eye . . . the wheels inside my head were really turning . . . what about the small print in my insurance cover? It probably wouldn't matter down here, nobody would ever know. My heartbeat increased three-fold.

With just a small filament globe for light, all four of us, including the stockily built Terry, moved to the end of a nearby drive. This was to be the face to blast. Any debris or rock from the previous blasting was removed with the help of a very powerful vacuum pump connected to a generator above ground. Now I know what a tarantula feels like when being sucked up by a vacuum cleaner.

The last time I had a brace 'n' bit in my hands must have been during my years as a student of architecture. But never one two metres long and 50-60 mm in diameter. It was double hernia material just to pick this one up. When I pressed the trigger, all the meat balls, pies, sandwiches and saveloys from the previous night hit 'rock bottom'.

Terry would have made a great orchardist. The symmetry of the freshly drilled nine holes in the stark rock face was excellent.

Terry and Peter said I could have the honour of lighting the first wick. Eighty seconds was all the time we had from the lighting of wick No. 1 to wick No. 9. By the 80 sec. mark the first big bang was guaranteed.

The tomcat's tail or wick dangling at my right hand side got my approval. Ideally I would light the fuse creating a spark and puff of smoke and pose for a picture at the same time. "Let's be bloody quick then and no second takes, okay!" was my firm answer.

With a mini-gas flame thrower in hand, I gingerly crouched in position . . . cameras, aim, action! Just as a fierce orange and yellow flame extended from my small oxy-acetylene type lighter, Peter, who placed himself directly behind me, pressed the trigger of the industrial jack-hammer he was leaning on. "Bzzzzzt tttbzztt!" I'm glad my trousers were tucked in — because scared was not the word!

I successfully lit the fuse. The small igniting device now took on the proportion of a relay runner's baton. A perfect change-over was effected from my right hand to a smirking Terry. The seconds were rapidly passing by . . . eventually all nine fuses alight. Pace was never one of my great attributes but I reached the safety of a faraway tunnel with 73 seconds to spare. I was terrified!

Some 40 seconds later the two 'pros' appeared in the tunnel looking very calm about proceedings. Fellow visitor Brian and I were told to put our earplugs in and brace ourselves for the explosion —Terry and Peter used only their index fingers, seeing that we had their plugs.

Boooom, Boom, Boom, Boom, Boom, Boooooom . . . the two visitors plus the effervescent Terry could only count eight bangs! "What now my friend"? It was a big question.

The percussion from the blasting had sent quite a substantial vibration from my toes to the top of my skull . . . it was an exceptionally unnerving experience. Silence reigned supreme. Just moments later a thick wall of brown dust caused by the explosion engulfed our bodies on its journey to the extremities of each tunnel or shaft. It took quite a while for the dust to settle as well as the colour to return to our faces.

Still, the problem remained — what happened to number nine? Did two go off simultaneously, in one sound or is there still one 'live bugger' left?

I wasn't about to volunteer going back into that rabbit warren full of rock and dust. Brian's eyes had 'NO' fully imprinted across the face of them. His eyebrows heavy with the burden of freshly landed red and white dust plus the urgency of the problem.

I laugh now, but it was deadly serious at the time. Many old timers have died in similar circumstances . . .

Terry, with the words, "I dig it mate", stretched across his T-shirt, decided everything was okay and ventured back into the silence of the doubtful tunnel.

He left with a poker face but returned with a flashing grin like the entry to Luna Park. "I don't know what you blokes were worried about, no problems, looking good!" he stated.

Brian and myself still weren't convinced, but we didn't want to look like squibs. Mind you, we could have also been dead heroes!

Ten minutes later all the fallen rock had been sucked to the surface and we were ready to dig opal — you bloody beauty!

I think at that precise point I was bitten by the bug. The possibility of finding a rare specimen of opalised fossil, or the like, felt a big chance. Adrenalin started to pump as my eyes bounced up and down the rockface . . .

After investigating the newly exposed wall, Peter began to dig with the noisy jackhammer. My turn came, and I found how energy-sapping it could be, but if I were to find a fossilised opal the size of a scallop shell, I suppose I'd feel no pain.

Well, I didn't find one and my shoulder was beginning to feel like a toothache. They were laughing — I was supposed to be fit.

The pick was like a toothpick by comparison, as I eased flakes of 'potch' from sedimentary layers above my head, not knowing what the next arc of the pick would prise away.

I was excited and wondering, if I found an opal, how would I get it out of the mine without them knowing!

The problem didn't eventuate, and back at Peter's dug-out, bags and bottles of cut and uncut opals were produced, with the scales. A couple of the gems caught my eye and I made a purchase or two. I only hope I have more luck than with my diamond and gold trading.

A Swinger hits the course

'I TOPPED THE SHOT AND SUCCEEDED ONLY IN HITTING THE CONCRETE KERB ON THE OTHER SIDE'

Golf is a game I would love to master! But like the rest of us mere mortals I lack both the ability and time to achieve that goal. In fact, until recently, the last round of golf I played must have been whilst I was attending a series of talks at the Arnhem Club in Gove at the northern extremity of the Northern Territory.

The tranquility of the newly-completed golf course was hard to beat — the old, oil-based, sand scrape 'greens' had just been replaced by flat, well

I knew they meant business when one of them hit my buggy hard and dislodged a five iron.

manicured grass. This was done so that the Gove Golf Club could host its own full scale Pro-Am tournament.

By the time I had reached the tee for the third hole, on the first day, I realised then that even though I wasn't bowling a cricket ball down the fairway, I still had the old ability to move the ball either way in the air! In other words I was hooking and slicing my drives, but not at will.

My No. 1 wood off the tee on the tird hole, was a huge "inswinger" which went so far into the rough, that I met three water buffaloes on the way in and then found six golf balls on the way out!

It was these same wild animals that had caused quite a deal of concern on the eve of the historic event . . . because a group of about four or five of these huge animals had decided to hold a number of 'team meetings' on the lush, green surfaces of the newly laid greens. The result was literally hundreds of hoof marks etched into the putting surface.

Now it's hard enough to get down in two putts at the best of times, but with these semi-circular depressions upsetting the normally level ground, it would have been almost impossible. Quick action was necessary.

Permission from the elder tribesmen amongst the local Aboriginal community was sought in order to kill the beasts concerned and thus eradicate the problem.

I had plenty of problems with my putter anyway and missed the cut.

The memories of that round came back to me later on as I stood above a tiny golf ball on the tee for the first hole at the Launceston Country Club course. The ball looked like an orange marble resting on top of a match stick and the No. 2 wood in my hands felt like a metal fishing line with a large sinker on the end of it.

This time I was playing a round, or should I say 'sharing' my limited golfing skills with Erik Scholz, the managing director of Dorf Industries (the tap people), and two other friends, Terry and David, who were both involved in the plumbing industry . . . which seemed pretty appropriate considering the golf course itself was waterlogged due to heavy rainfall overnight.

The huge lake some 50 metres ahead of our tee-off position looked and felt almost magnetic — something I couldn't say about the hired size 11 golf shoes! They felt like size 13s, or a couple of boats with metal spikes in the underside for steering — a touch of Ben Lexcen about the design of these dark tan beauties! Nevertheless, they gave me the confidence to go and get my ball in the watery lies without danger of getting tinea.

The object of the day was to hit the ball over the lake and any water hazards, not into them. The first "plop!" into the murky water, punctured by long, slender reeds, brought forth a loud round of laughter . . . maybe it was just a release of some nervous energy or even a pleasant relief that it wasn't my ball in the drink. Then the second and third balls went in. The fourth one sent up a tall spray like Halley's Comet as it careered across the surface.

The skimpy set of clubs we had each hired didn't help our game either

— our choice was limited to a No. 2 wood, 3 iron, 5 iron, 7 iron, sand wedge and putter. They were actually acknowledged on a sign in the club house as being similar to those that the 'Great White Shark', Greg Norman, uses.

Well, I can honestly tell you that even Greg Norman would be flat out hitting a sub-par round with these little numbers — they'd certainly played a few rounds before I got them in my sweaty palms.

By the time my group arrived at the fifth tee I was really enjoying myself. That was obvious to see judging by the amount of mud on my pale corduroy trousers which were finally tucked into my socks. It looked a little like the knickerbocker style of the old boys at the turn of the century.

My badly hooked, full-blooded drive got me into plenty of strife on this hole because the ball bounced off the hard bitumen road which was a long way left of the nice fairway! The ball finally came to rest in some very large tractor treads leading from a nearby building site.

I thought it fair to treat it as G.U.R. or ground under repair, so I dropped the ball out a club length or two — what's a club length or two between friends when you're that far from the pin? Just my luck, the ball dropped 'plop' into a pile of cow dung. "Get it out of this stuff in one hit Maxie," I thought to myself.

My selection was an elevated seven iron so that the ball would clear the road and position itself in a good lie on the fairway. No such luck. I topped the shot and succeeded only in hitting the concrete kerb on the other side of the road which deflected the ball back towards where I was still rather gingerly standing, nostrils filled with the stench of the fresh cow dung, which had splattered on impact. Eventually the ball stopped about 60 metres away against a cigarette box in the dirty gutter. Again it was not a good lie!!!

So, once more I bent the rules, as time was rushing by. This time I dropped the ball on to the adjacent nature strip and then with the class of Arnold Palmer, yours truly cleared the road, a cluster of trees, a bunker and dropped the iron shot about five metres off the flag. You little beauty!! When you're running hot I guess your're running hot because the putt also fell in!

Amongst a lot of ordinary shots and a few good ones, we turned the corner on to the back nine — had I been playing cricket my score of 47 not out then would have been very pleasing.

All four of us continued to apply our knowledge of hot and cold taps and running water to the fullest. We played in and out of one water hazard after another.

Then suddenly I was attacked by several low flying plovers. These local birds are about the same size of magpies but have spurs under their wings to make them quite dangerous. I knew they meant business when one of them hit my buggy hard and dislodged a five iron, whilst I was addressing the ball. I'm sure these very confident birds must have been home trained just to make life more interesting for guys like us when almost in sight of the 18th hole.

I pulled away from the ball so that I would not get struck by my feathered friends. Above my head the singing three iron was starting to look like the rotor of a Channel 9 helicopter about to take off for a news story as I shooed away the attackers.

When we eventually did walk through the door of the club house to hand in our shoes, clubs, and the three balls each of us hadn't used, it made me realise just how talented the great players of this world are . . . they deserve every penny they can earn.

We exchanged those three new unsoiled golf balls for 95 cents each. They immediately went into the secondhand bucket of balls on sale at $1 each. Not bad, eh? Considering we originally bought them for $1.50 each and they were still brand new.

It's a funny game golf, and I look forward to my next round . . . without the plovers and water hazards.

Hanging on for dear life
'SOME PASSENGERS, I'M TOLD, RETURNED WHITE AND SPEECHLESS'

About the most fearsome thing I've ever faced in my life was a little red missile fired by the giant West Indian fast bowler Joel Garner — at around 90 miles per hour. Well, that was before I got caught up with husband and wife driving team, David and Kate Officer.

They were preparing themselves to tackle the 1986 Australian Rally Championship in their magnificent new Mitsubishi Starion.

Somehow I managed to get dragged into one of their practice sessions, at the Melbourne Showgrounds.

My reason for talking to David, the 1984 winner of the national title, was part of an assignment for National Nine News. I left Channel 9 Studios in Richmond with a film crew just as I'd done many times before, but little did I know what the next hour or so would hold . . .

If my commitment to the story was only to ask a few well chosen questions and then let the camera crew capture some great pictures, everything would have been fine, but this was not to be. The key to making this exercise a success was for yours truly to do a few laps with the rally champ.

To be honest, the closest I'd been to a ride in a rally car prior to this fateful day was sitting down every Saturday afternoon and watching the highlights of some of the world's top rally events on *Wide World of Sports*. And after witnessing plenty of hair-raising action from the contestants, I was more than happy just being a spectator.

Also, in the back of my mind were a few stories I'd heard about some of our best racing car drivers taking people for a spin around the circuit with the specific intention of frightening the living daylights out of them. Some

126

passengers, I'm told, returned white and speechless — particularly television reporters!

Well, as I always say, no guts no glory. Let's have a go!

Dave and his wife seemed a nice enough couple as I asked them a few questions. In fact, their enthusiasm to speak about the new car was similar to a kid with a new toy. "It's a better car than our previous one. This one's powered by a Sirius 2.0 litre turbo charged, fuel injected engine, producing 250 brake horsepower.

"The car itself was completely stripped and rebuilt by David and Brian Smith. The car is fully seam welded and has an integral roll cage. Also the suspension has been upgraded to cope with the tough demands of rallying on forest roads. Full harness-type seat belts are used in the body hugging seats. And most importantly, all crew have to wear safety helmets!"

Maybe that was a hint of the danger ahead but I was very pleased to put one on. Actually it looked a lot like the prototype crash helmet that cricketer Tony Greig used to use in the early days of Kerry Packer's World Series Cricket.

I should mention that Greig's helmet was continually being taken to the panel beaters to knock out the dents where fast bowlers Dennis Lillee and Lennie Pascoe kept hitting it!

After fastening the strap of my helmet, I awkwardly folded my big frame into the left hand seat of the tiny cabin. There wasn't a great deal of room left after the installation of the roll cage. My knees were almost up around my chin as David reached for the ignition . . . I was having trouble with my harness seatbelt . . . it needed letting out quite a bit. I certainly am a lot bigger than David's wife Kate.

My heart was starting to pound loudly as the turbo-charged engine barked under the bonnet.

I was told to watch my head as we took off — it was already touching the roof and made a spine-chilling sound as helmet scraped against metal!

We were up and running on the sandy trotting track, dust spitting out from the rotating, soft chunky tread tyres used specially for this type of surface. Harder tyres are used on surfaces like stone and bitumen. In fact one set of rear tyres are worn out every 20-30 kilometres in competitive rallying . . . that's really burning rubber.

As we hit the first bend much faster than I would expected, my appetite for rally driving deteriorated — my life was now in the hands of David Officer and I knew the next few minutes weren't going to be pleasant.

We were tackling the track anti-clockwise, not that it was really relevant to how my stomach was feeling . . . gee, I was glad I hadn't had a greasy breakfast such as bacon and eggs! They may have ended up on the dashboard!!!

Apparently, in some instances, the effect of the unorthodox motion of the car zig-zagging its way through the course and with trees flashing by, is bad car sickness for the navigator who is attempting to give the driver the 'good oil' on where they're going. And in a rally there's no chance to stop the car on the side of the road. If it's a long stage, it could be quite a sickening experience, not to mention smelly.

I think the only thing preventing me from using a couple of very common expletives was the fact that I had a microphone clipped onto my tie. Even that was a sore point. Imagine wearing a tie to go rally driving — definitely overdressed!

At this stage I looked and felt everything but a rally navigator . . . I was too busy looking for a crash rail I desperately wanted to hang on to. No such luck, it had to be the underside of the seat. I could feel the muscles in my face tense up — not to mention the ones in my buttocks. My eyes couldn't have been deeper in their sockets. My back firmly gravitated into the upright section of the body hugging seat.

As for the control of the car . . . I was hoping David wasn't trying too hard to impress me with the handling capabilities. He assured me he wasn't going too fast into the bends and besides there was nothing to crash into here . . . not like driving through a forest on a muddy road or on a mountain edge where the road is covered with ice.

I watched his hands working overtime to control the sliding rear end of the growling Starion. It seemed we were almost travelling the entire circuit sideways — compensating only slightly in the short straight lengths of the track.

I've been frightened a few times in my life but this was different — everything was out of my control. Sort of like a big dipper ride but on the flat, except my stomach was going up and down, not yet out of control, but not really feeling too flash.

The braking of the car has a forward and rear bias, something I guessed was pretty important . . . too much brake would be a bit like too much oversteer — you'd lose control of the car.

It was a nerve-wracking experience, one I shall never forget. When you hop in beside a champion like David Officer it gives a great appreciation of the incredible skills of these drivers.

For the uninitiated, the modern rally is basically a race against the clock on a series of closed forest roads (called special stages). A stage can run in length from 2 km to 100 km, although the average these days is about 20 km.

Each crew commences a stage at two-minute intervals, and is timed to the second. The least cumulative time taken over all the stops decides the stage. And the least cumulative time taken over all the stages decides the winner.

Events are typically won and lost by very small margins, often less than a second per kilometre of stage distance. Consequently rally driving is an extremely competitive sport — a lapse of concentration, a wrong tyre choice, or a slight mistake, can mean the difference between a win and a loss.

The course is secret until the actual start of the event, and is read out to the driver by the navigator, who must concentrate 100 per cent of the time, because any missed instructions can have massive repercussions!

This is where David's wife comes in. She's the one with all that responsibility, but Kate can handle it — she has the distinction of being the first woman to win a national motor sports event.

The navigator is also responsible for calculating fuel and tyre stop intervals and also directing the service crew to locations where the competing vehicle will meet them.

Gee I was pleased when we stopped and in style . . . a 180 degree handbrake stop — sand and dust everywhere as we broadsided in front of the cameraman.

I felt a lot better after talking to one of David's maintenance crew, Andy Brown. We got talking about car sickness and he said: "Mate, the most bullet proof blokes I've seen have been reduced to a puddle of grease after a ride in one of these.

The sky's the limit

'I HAD VISIONS OF SOMEONE — HOPEFULLY NOT ME — BEING SUCKED OUT OF THE OPEN DOOR'

"We all ought to be certified for getting back into this bastard of a plane!" shouted Sam Newman from the rear of our temporary prison. For surely, we were doing time the hard way — trapped in a tiny flying machine.

Sam, the former Geelong VFL footballer and then a Melbourne television sports personality, was sharing the second, or back row, of a four-seater, twin-engine Cessna next to notorious Melbourne television character, Peter 'Crackers' Keenan, a veteran of more than 250 games with VFL clubs Melbourne, North Melbourne and Essendon.

Yours truly was in the cramped cockpit — in the seat reserved for the co-pilot. From the beginning, I had been almost hypnotised by the glaring mass of illuminated green and yellow gauges before my eyes.

Graeme, our young pilot, was responsible for safely transporting Sam, Crackers and myself to and from a speaking engagement in the small town of Cohuna, in the north of Victoria.

The small aircraft was being buffeted continually, like a lost balloon, in strong wind gusts. The plane had just fallen abruptly — about 1000 feet — when Sam made his timely comment.

Crackers and I agreed, and he replied quickly: "Gee, I feel close to God, but I don't want to meet him just yet!"

It wasn't exactly a religious happening, but the time we shared in that cramped, dark interior of the plane certainly was soul searching stuff! I kept thinking about what a terrible bloke I'd been all my life . . . and how I might live if ever I got another chance!

I've got it on pretty good authority that there was some good money within the four of us to say that we would not get back to ground in one piece! And I'm not telling any lies when I say we were all very bloody frightened. Maybe it was the bad beginning to our epic journey?

What a way to start! As we calmly taxied down the black bitumen tarmac, there was very little discussion, other than the preceding week's events. At near top speed, our wheels left the tarmac of Essendon airport.

A perfect take-off I thought. Sammy and Crackers didn't really care as they dissected VFL footballers' recent performances. Whatever the sport, old players never die, they just become experts in their sport, or maybe commentators like myself, eh?

"Bloody hell!" Sam screamed, as we were barely 300 ft above the ground, and still climbing, because the pilot's door flew open. Wind at about 160 kmh gushed into the cockpit. My heart began pounding very loudly — I was terrified! And I know that I wasn't an orphan in feeling like that!

I flung my left arm across the pilot's back, like any 'great' slips fieldsman might, to grab the flapping door. Simultaneously, both hands from the 6'4" ruckman from Geelong appeared from the other direction, desperately trying to pull the door shut.

Crackers was issuing the obvious instruction at the top of his voice: "Shut the bloody door, quick shut it, c'mon Sam shut it!"

The door would not close, despite superhuman efforts by Sam and me.

Through all this, the pilot was huddled grim-faced over the aeroplane's controls to give us a better chance to slam the door.

The lights of Essendon were all too bright below us — barely 500 ft off the ground. For some reason, the door still would not slam shut after several more vigorous attempts. Graeme struggled with the joy stick as we banked steeply round the control tower.

At one stage, I reckon we must have been flying side-ways at 90 degrees to Earth and hanging on for grim death. I felt the long legs of Peter Pius Paul Keenan almost pushed through the back of my seat as he fought the forces of gravity.

A unanimous decision was made to land the plane and see what was wrong — who said footballers had no brains? On this occasion, commonsense prevailed!

I had visions of someone — hopefully not me — being sucked out the open door into the cold dark night air, never to be seen again! Just like in the film *Airport '75*.

The very large lump in my throat had moved and lodged somewhere near the back of my ears as we levelled out over the Tullamarine freeway ... if only we can land this plane safely?

I should not have doubted Graeme's ability, for we came in for a smooth landing. We were right back where we started five minutes earlier.

Without even stopping the plane, the door was much easier to close when we were rolling slowly along the tarmac. I wonder why?

Nerves frayed, but confidence restored, we powered down the runway for the second time. Crackers suggested that the air traffic controller in the tower may have believed he was drunk seeing the same plane take off twice in seven minutes. It was good to hear humour again!

But it didn't last long as we struggled into very strong headwinds. We should have been travelling at 160 knots, instead we were averaging only 105.

Long before we reached Bendigo, we agreed that it was the worst flight we had been on, except for Graeme, who was showing a brave face.

Then the small charter plane pressed forward relentlessly into the face of a very nasty storm. Thunder punctuated the unhealthy silence inside, while outside heavy rain pelted the windscreen, and lightning forks etched golden lines into the night. Visibility could have been barely 10 metres —we truly were flying blind.

Graeme would not dare let his hands leave the controls as we continually dropped out of the sky with devastating effects on my stomach, which had become knotted.

Our plane was taking a battering in appalling conditions — it was a real effort to fly horizontally.

We were told that sick bags were in the seat pockets. I was too scared to be sick, while Crackers said that if he was going to be sick, then it was only right the pilot should wear it. From where I sat it looked more like I would wear it.

I should mention too that Crackers had been to lunch: and garlic prawns had been on the menu. Every time he opened his mouth it was like a garlic flame thrower. The plane's interior was beginning to smell like an oven full of garlic bread. Very selfish that . . . I'll get him . . . but it did take our minds from our dangerous situation.

My palms were very sweaty, and I believe that the giant ruckmen may have been holding hands as we plummetted through the clouds.

The rain on the wings now looked like huge sparks illuminated by the flashing wing lights — they were heavy drops pounding on the windscreen.

I never have felt so insecure for such a long time! The two lads in the back were joking nervously about the possible news stories if we went down. A lot of those little planes do!

Something along the line of: "Football will miss Peter Keenan and Sam Newman, the two VFL champion footballers tragically killed with their friend, former Test cricketer Max Walker, when their light aircraft crashed north of Bendigo last night on its way to a speaking engagement at Cohuna."

As funny as it may sound, it could have been all too true! Nevertheless, we exchanged versions like jokes — I don't think our pilot was impressed. But I'm sure he realised our grave situation. As Crackers said: "Don't worry Maxie, he's a mature 21-year-old."

I thought here we are, our lives in the hands of a fragile, metal machine with two props and a 21-year-old pilot. Unreal, and for what? A few hundred dollars for the night.

But it soon was established that we were getting three times the amount the pilot was getting — absolutely insane!

Graeme could have been at home watching telly for that money — mind you, so could we! Sam said: "How far is it to Cohuna, 1¼ hours? We've been going for 1½ hours and haven't looked like making bloody Cohuna!"

"Yeah." Crackers said impatiently, "we should've driven up — could have saved a few bob and a lot of heartache!"

Finally, almost two hours after our original take-off, we were in the vicinity of our flight destination, Kerang. We were flying at about 4500 ft, give or take a thousand feet depending on the clouds and rain. All we had to do was find the airstrip — not easy!

I watched the altimeter spin from 4600 ft to well below 1000 ft — still no sign of the strip. My ears popped and I hung on tight, hoping there was no radio tower or mountain tucked away secretly in the darkness below us.

Then, from nowhere, the two parallel blue lines appeared to our right — I didn't think that two parallel blue lines could look so good. We did one arbitrary lap of honour before we made our final approach to land.

The nervous tension had got to us — we all started laughing as Graeme again put us on deck with a beautiful landing in pouring rain.

While the propellers unwound, and our aeroplane came to a standstill, I thought: no way am I getting back into this kite, unless we've got clear skies. Judging by the amount of water bouncing off the wings it looked like overnight at Cohuna.

You are not going to believe me when I tell you this, but about 12.30 a.m. we left Kerang in clear skies. But around Bendigo we hit the storms again and sat through the same fear for another hour.

We could not get Graeme to admit that it was the worst flying conditions he had flown in. But he did describe them "as a long way way from the best!"

I can understand why people hate small aircraft or even flying — you feel so helpless! Never again!

Chapter Six

A FUNNY THING HAPPENED ON THE WAY TO . . .

His big brown eyes pleaded for at least a hearing.

In the dark over diamonds
'HIS HEAD ROTATED LEFT AND RIGHT LIKE A MINIATURE RADAR ANTENNA'

As a rule, Australian cricketers on tour have been notoriously bad negotiators where value for money was concerned. A wonderful example of just how bad occurred in Johannesburg during Richie Benaud's International Wanderers Tour of South Africa in 1976.

We had just completed a 'Test match' against an invitation multi-racial South African XI containing players of the calibre of Barry Richards, Graeme Pollock, Eddie Barlow and Clive Rice.

The huge Wanderers Stadium had been the venue for the game. It was an especially memorable occasion for Martin Kent who scored a belligerent 155 for his maiden international century, while Dennis Lillee took seven wickets in the second innings. Graeme Pollock also reeled off a century in their first innings.

Both Ashley 'Rowdy' Mallett and myself had the pleasure of our wives' company on this trip. Needless to say the girls had organised a shopping expedition at the first available chance after the game.

Armed with both credit cards and some cash we soon found ourselves in the heart of downtown Johannesburg. What little cash our wives had was burning a hole in their pockets. I knew it was just a matter of time before a bargain would jump out of a shop window and grab our money. I wasn't wrong!

Strangely enough the first opportunity came in the form of a very dark native man who appeared from behind a very bushy tree in the plaza area of the new Carlton Towers Complex — a very contemporary architectural design of three sterile grey concrete towers enclosing the central space.

As it turned out, the trees, in huge concrete tubs, were the perfect cover for characters like the little man now standing in our pathway.

His big brown eyes pleaded for at least a hearing, as he moved positively toward us like an alert watchdog. Judging by the elbow in my ribs I knew my wife Tina wanted nothing to do with the fellow. Alongside me Ashley was also getting similar pressure to ignore the offer.

He was a short, stocky black man dressed in a very dirty old grey suit — I'm sure he'd not washed for a week. In his hand, through his grubby fingers, I could see a small blue velvet ring box.

"You buy diamond, sir?" he whispered as his head rotated left and right like a miniature radar antenna, obviously with a view to an early departure should one of the local constabulary see him soliciting us.

Curiosity got the better of Rowdy and myself — I professing to know all there was to know about diamonds, having made a purchase the previous year whilst on tour with the Derrick Robins XI in South Africa.

Yes, I had bought a diamond ring for my wife, as did several other

135

players, one of whom got a blister on his little toe because he believed that was his best chance of getting through Customs without declaring his jewels . . . another story that one!

After a brief chat it was agreed we should at least look at the man's offering — so a meeting was set up under very clandestine conditions.

The location was to be outside the clothes store, just around the corner, in 10 minutes' time.

Some colourful clothing had attracted the attention of our wives and they were soon engrossed in trying on a selection of garments on the first floor of the same fashion shop.

Meanwhile Rowdy and myself rendezvoused with the 'super salesman' as planned. After a short interrogation, it was discovered that he worked for a jeweller and this was his lunch hour. A likely story, but his manner was convincing.

The unveiling occurred without delay in the shade of the shop canopy and a screen of thick horizontal landscaping. Even then we were given only a very quick glimpse of the contents — a diamond engagement ring setting with an accompanying matching wedding ring, beautifully displayed in the white silk interior of that tiny blue velvet box.

We called 'time out' for a private discussion. This sent the African's head swivelling like a ventriloquist's doll as he anxiously feared for his well being.

My educated guess was — a diamond just over 1 carat worth may be $2500 — Rowdy was ecstatic! I suggested we both go into partnership 50 per cent each and pay up to 50 Rand for it.

Not good enough for Ashley — he was adamant that he be the sole trader and 100 per cent shareholder. I didn't show my disappointment, yet inwardly I believed I'd done enough to share the profits. You see we were going bring the 'rock' back to Australia and sell it on the open market . . . we thought it that good.

Our next and most important question was ready or not: "Prove it's a diamond!" I said. Rowdy threatened not to buy the merchandise if he could not prove it. As any diamond trader knows — diamonds can cut or scratch glass.

That apparently was sufficient encouragement to send our man into immediate action. He rushed over to the enormous plate glass shop window, continuously peering over his shoulder so as not to be seen. He than beckoned us to witness first hand his diamond.

It all happened too quickly for me — yet sure enough he was untroubled in making two deep gashes in the tinted glass facade.

That was it . . . I said, "Rowdy it definitely is a real bloody diamond, just look at those scratches!" I could sense the off-spinner's excitement as he grinned back.

The 'diamond trader' by this stage was becoming impatient and irritated. There remained only to effect the monetary transaction and the deal was clinched. The little bloke said, "Call me George" and requested we continue our debate on this fantastic bargain somewhere else. "Too many people here!" he pleaded.

On the other side of the plaza, secure behind two more bushy plants, we met again to finalise our arrangement. Rowdy played it very hard and to the point, battering the price from 135 Rand to 37 Rand even given the guy had two hungry children to feed, or so he said.

Now Ashley Mallett is no Stephen Spielberg but produced his super 8mm movie camera to record the historic deal. Rowdy became the cameraman as I nervously fumbled the 37 Rand from my mate's tattered leather wallet. It must have been riveting footage but will it ever get shown I wonder?

No sooner had George gloved the 37 Rand than he was gone like a cheetah over the horizon.

Extremely proud of his purchase, Rowdy suggested showing the diamond haul to his wife Chris, who by this time was just zipping up the fifth pair of denim jeans she'd tried on.

Her reaction was completely unexpected. She told him he was bloody mad and should not waste their hard earned money.

Rowdy said unashamedly that he would return at least 1000 per cent on his investment.

Tina was also strong on the criticism and chastised me for my involvement. Nevertheless I backed my mate to the hilt as you would expect. After all what are mates for?

Inside the jeweller's shop on the way back to our hotel, we anxiously awaited the expert's word on our bargain. Rather stern-faced the big blonde Afrikaans jeweller said, "Maybe the wedding ring is worth 12 Rand but the engagement setting . . . no more than 75 cents! Both plastic fakes!" he said. You've been had!"

At this stage the man behind the counter couldn't help himself from smiling . . . I burst into laughter and Chris wasted no time in telling Rowdy "I told you so! You stupid . . . !"

It just goes to show how luck intervenes, eh? By not being hungry for potential profit I missed out on a 50 per cent share of 12.75 Rand for an investment of 18.50 Rand.

I'm laughing all the way to the bank. And all dear Ashley has is the transaction in full color Super 8 Cinemascope to remember the occasion by — bless his heart!

Death of the President's dog
'LILLEE RETURNED BRUSHING DOWN HIS JUMPER AND COMPLAINING ABOUT THE BLOODSTAINS'

A series of events during the 1973 Australian tour of the West Indies had us in stitches of laughter even if they did cause some of the locals a slight embarrassment. This story really should be known as the tale of the

President's dog, and not surprisingly centres around that irrepressible character D.K. Lillee.

Although that tour was not a happy one for Dennis — he suffered a severe back injury which put him out of cricket for more than a year — he certainly did his bit to give the boys some comic relief off the field.

Lillee had developed a stunt which involved scaring the daylights out of the drivers who ferried us around in the team bus.

The buses we used had wooden slatted seats and no windows. In fact, very tinny conveyances all round.

One day our driver had been manoeuvring to squeeze the bus through large gate pillars, with plenty of encouragement from the lads.

Dennis leaned out of the window and nearly belted a hole in the red metal panelling with his fist. The sound was like a bomb exploding, and someone yelled "You've hit the bloody post you stupid fool!"

The poor driver slammed on the brakes, stalled the bus and was quickly out of the seat and around to inspect the damage, looking as if he was to face an execution squad for his folly. Of course he couldn't understand why there was still a good six inches of clearance between the bus and the post when he had clearly heard a crash.

Eventually he began to get the message, and even saw the funny side.

On another occasion when we were on a shopping expedition, Lillee and the same bus driver cooked up a bit of a stunt between them.

A very old jalopy was parked in the spot where the bus driver was supposed to be, so Lillee persuaded the driver to drive as fast as possible at the old wreck, pull up with a squeal of the motor and scream of tyres.

As he did so, Lillee and a couple of the others were out of the bus peering at the 'damage' to the jalopy and of course berating our driver for his 'carelessness'.

This display caused the driver to laugh until the tears ran down his cheeks and he was laughing all the harder when out of the jalopy stepped two nuns in full regalia.

Suddenly the humour of the affair had disappeared for our man Lillee — and we saw no more of his favorite trick for quite a while.

One night however he decided it was about time for a comeback.

It was another of those tedious official functions that cricketers around the world have to endure. I can't even remember which island it was on, but I'm sure it was the President who threw this particular cocktail party. I know it was after a long hot day's cricket and we didn't have time to have a meal beforehand.

Cricketers get a bit blase about these functions. They are rather like hotels — once through the door you could be anywhere in the world.

But the setting for this party was extraordinary. We drove in through an enormous, white ornate gateway and along a driveway that seemed to stretch for a mile.

The house — it was more like a palace — was fronted with Corinthian columns and a huge flight of white marble steps led up to a doorway even more ornate than the gates.

Inside, there were vaulted ceilings towering 20 feet above us and the function was held in a ballroom that came straight out of a Hollywood musical extravaganza.

As usual there were servants moving among the guests with paper thin sardine sandwiches curled up at the edges and the drink was flowing like the Amazon.

But we were hungry and a group of us — team manager Bill Jacobs, Dennis Lillee, Greg Chappell, Kerry O'Keeffe, and myself decided to take up an invitation from the Australian Trade Commissioner for a few drinks and some good old Aussie pies and sauce out at his residence.

Our transport that night happened to be a company by the name of Taboo Taxis.

We woke the driver from his slumber and gave him directions to the Trade Commissioner's house. It was as we approached the two white stone pillars of the gateway that D.K. Lillee made his play.

He put his arm out of the window and gave the outside of the door a very heavy thump. Then he turned poker-faced and told the startled driver, "Look what you've done — you've run over the President's dog."

Then he was out bending over the front wheel yowling for all the world like a dying dog. The noises were realistically blood-curdling. Lillee, shielded by the darkness kept up the mimickry. Then he carried the 'body' over to a culvert as the 'dog' gave its last gasp.

Lillee returned brushing down his jumper and complaining about the bloodstains. Greg Chappell intervened with his voice very serious too. "You'll have to go back and tell the President what you've done to his dog."

"I can't do that man," the driver wailed. "I've got a wife and six kids."

He had gone Persil white under his sun-tan.

"Then let's get the hell out of here," Lillee suggested.

We shot out on to the main road which must have been all of 20 ft wide and were making good time when Lillee struck again.

"Watch out for that dog!" he shouted.

There was a wild screech of brakes, the cab slewed sideways and the driver sat there quivering. "Hey man I didn't see nothing," he moaned.

"You didn't?" Lillee sounded incredulous. "It was a big black one. It ran right across the road in front of you. You only missed him by an inch."

Twice more in the next couple of miles there was a re-enactment of the scene. Lillee yelling, car slewing, driver perspiring and near to the point of collapse.

After the third incident we proceeded at a much more cautious pace and as luck would have it, the first lamp post we came to had a black and white spotted dog sitting at its base.

About 200 yards from it the driver dropped right through the gears back to first and crawled along at about half a mile an hour, all the time watching the dog for all he was worth.

Once past, he accelerated like a rocket into the night. The problem now was we had got the driver such a state of shock that he was thoroughly lost. We had no idea of where we should be heading. We talked him into stopping at a run-down shanty shop to seek directions.

As we slowed down, a very old grey-haired fellow was alighting from an equally old push bike. The old bloke propped it up on the kerb as our cab pulled in close behind.

Lillee gave the outside of the door a further clout and lo and behold the bike fell over of its own accord!

Dennis was immediately out of the car pretending to push the rear wheel of the bike back into shape watched by the old gentleman whose eyes were standing out like light globes.

Inside the cab the driver was getting a real bawling out, "You've hit the bloke's bike. It'll cost a fortune to fix. Are you drivers all blind?"

At that moment another car arrived on the scene. By sheer coincidence it was the Trade Commissioner. He stopped abruptly with puzzlement all over his face.

Bill Jacobs was quickly over to the other car explaining our little game to the Trade Commissioner.

He immediately entered into the spirit of the affair. He strode around to the front of the cab peered into the window and said: "I want to see your licence, driver."

The driver was in an absolute panic. He turned out his pockets, emptied the glove box . . . but no licence.

All the while he was telling the Commissioner how poor he was, and how he had to support 12 children (amazing how the number doubled in half an hour!) Not to mention what a law abiding citizen he was.

The Commissioner began to lecture the poor fellow on the seriousness of knocking down bicycles, but presumably he was getting as peckish as we were, because he brought the show to an end by instructing him to follow his car to the 'station' where the matter would be more fully investigated.

He then led the way to his palatial home on a hill overlooking the city. Anything less like a West Indies police station would be difficult to imagine. There the driver received another lecture and the Commissioner mentioned that another matter had come to his attention — that of the President's dog.

This brought forth a torrent of apologies from the hapless driver and a promise that nothing like it would ever happen again.

The poor fellow was sent on his way but his ordeal was not over yet because the house was in a narrow dead-end street, and the cab had to go to the end, do a three-point turn and then come back past us.

Never one to let any opportunity slip Dennis grabbed hold of a lemon from a nearby tree and as the cab drew level he let fly scoring a direct hit on the front mudguard.

For a fraction of a second the brakes were applied, then the driver stepped on the accelerator and the cab vanished in a whirl of blue smoke.

I don't remember much about the beer and pies, but I'll never forget that cab driver. And I have a suspicion that he'll never forget us!

No tomorrow in the air
'SHE TOLD ME THAT SHE HAD JUST GIVEN HERSELF TO SATAN!'

The stench inside the cabin of the old fashioned DC3 was sickening as the plane's two engines roared loudly. Outside, the temperature must have been near 40 deg. C and the humidity about a sticky 98 per cent.

There was no such thing as air conditioning once the pilot closed the door! Also the seating was fairly basic: a bit like a tram. The two middle seats about half-way down the fuselage were positioned so that two rows of passengers sat facing each other . . . and that's where the problem began.

We'd only just turned at the head of the airstrip on the magnificent tropical island of Tobago. Our destination on the LIAT flight was Trinidad, where Australia was to play its next cricket match during the 1973 tour of the West Indies.

Sitting next to me was my room-mate, former Australian leg-spinner Kerry O'Keeffe. Diagonally opposite me sat a little old lady, aged about 55

141

and skin as black as the ace of spades. Her face was etched with pain and discomfort.

We hadn't even taken off . . . it may have been her first flight . . . the tension of the occasion had got to her. Together with the strong petrol fumes wafting inside the cabin, it was enough to make her violently sick.

Right before our eyes, she'd taken off her beautiful straw boater-style hat with imitation cherries and red ribbon and was sick into it. We had no hosties, so both she and the rest of us were stuck with her delightful 'hat-trick' for the next 1½ hours. I thought, gee, are we going to be in trouble if the capacity of the poor woman's hat is not enough.

The journey was barely 15 minutes old when two members of our touring party had a dry retch or 'gentle spit' as they would have us believe — it's the worst flight I've ever sat through. Nearly the whole cabin full of passengers was air sick during the journey.

And all because of one little ol' lady and a badly upset tummy.

Add to this was a couple of big West Indian fellas wearing bri-nylon shirts and sweating profusely. By the smell of 'em, they hadn't had a tub for a week, either. Stale perspiration isn't too flash at the best of times.

The most challenging aspect of air travel is that you never quite know who you're going to sit next to. The mind boggles at the possibilities, especially overseas.

The person next to you could be what I call a 'Black & Decker drill' — someone who doesn't take a breath and will not stop asking the most stupid questions. These types are very easily recognisable — they're like a tape-recorder, with a new set of batteries. Hard to shut up!

The best way to overcome one of these characters is to go to sleep while he's talking to you, then just as the plane touches down wake up! Then humbly apologise for going to sleep half-way through a sentence . . . it works all the time.

I usually ask for a non-smoking seat, but they're not always available. Chain-smokers are the worst — continually blowing smoke at you from short range.

In 1977 on the way to England, I got stuck between Dougie Walters and Jeff Thomson —two of Australia's cricketing greats.

Our Qantas jumbo 747 had barely lifted off the ground when Dougie hit the hostess call button, and they simultaneously lit up cigarettes. Down came the card table as the smiling stewardess arrived and the first drink was ordered. It was the beginning of a long flight.

For the next 20 hours, I had smoke blown at me from both sides — my eyes felt as though they were full of sand. My clothes had a nasty odour of smoke and any amount of beer that got emptied over me in the persistent dealing of cards.

Doug Walters had a pretty fair trip . . . 100 cigarettes in 24 hours and 39 cans of beer in the flight time. No need to suggest how bad the floor of the cocky's cage was on arriving in London. But not nearly as bad as the headache Rodney Marsh carried with him off the plane at Heathrow (44 cans).

There are times, too, when you really get a 'live one' sitting next to you.

On the way back from Brisbane last year, I was sitting beside a 19-year-old girl dressed in jeans. My assessment was: a bit scruffy, but I should have a chat. At this stage, I didn't realise how jumpy she was . . . she kept rubbing her thighs and folding her arms at a frantic rate. Her eyes constantly focused on the black bitumen tarmac as we stayed in a line of five big jets waiting for the control tower to give them authority to take-off.

I asked the young lady if she was nervous or was it her first flight. No, she was going home to Portland, Victoria.

Nevertheless, she was very anxious — unusually so! I thought she may have been on drugs or something, so I checked out the inside of her arm for tinea or pin pricks. But clean as a whistle.

Before we were airborne, she'd produced a cigarette . . . fasten seat belt and no smoking signs were illuminated. She asked me for a light. Apart from being a non-smoking seat, I'd be the last bloke to ask for a light. The take-off was rough and turbulent. This caused her to shred her cigarette tobacco everywhere.

I could sense her problem of needing a 'puff' so I organised for her to go to the rear of the cabin for relief.

When she lobbed back in her seat, I tried the older brother approach or 'Dear Dorothy Dix', and I was shocked to hear of her dilemma.

She told me that she had just given herself to Satan . . . can you imagine how I felt! I'm not a big wrap for discussing politics and religion, let alone Satan!

But briefly, she'd followed her man to the Sunshine Coast expecting an idyllic life on a yacht sailing up and down the Great Barrier Reef.

He was part of a religious sect and — no yacht in sight — she was scared stiff at the prospect of facing her parents again after running away.

I tried to suggest that we all make mistakes and that tomorrow she was a new day, but it didn't work. She was still convinced that Satan had taken her soul and there may have been no tomorrow.

She'd already had to choose between her lover and his religious group. Then between him and her parents, Queensland or Victoria . . . she really was a confused young woman.

It was an enlightening flight to say the least.

Generally, cabin crews are great! That is until they spill coffee all over your light beige trousers with the cutest smile. What can a guy say when he's almost lost his equipment and got the bonus of a big brown stain as well, especially when you're meeting people, for the first time. Somehow they don't look you in the eye when they say, "Hello!" Or pick up the wrong suit carrier on the way off as happened recently.

It was a Saturday morning flight from Melbourne to Sydney to co-host the Channel 9 Wide World Of Sports show beginning at 1 p.m.

I didn't realise what had happened until about 12.40 p.m. . . . only 20 minutes before the program went to air. Having completed the scripting for the show, I headed off towards make-up feeling confident about the show, only to find I had somebody else's suit carrier.

My specially made 46 long WWOS blazer was nowhere to be found, neither was my XXOS shirt and hand-picked tie . . . they could have been anywhere . . . Brisbane, Townsville, Cairns!

I checked out the similar suit bag only to find two tiny brown suits and a pair of silk knickers and very brief at that! Naturally, everyone at the sports hut was fascinated by the panties, and before long they ended up as a practical joke on some unsuspecting guy's desk.

My problem still wasn't solved — no shirt, no coat and no tie. Producer Saul Stein was pretty emotional about it and I explained that it wasn't helping me to get an outfit together.

We did go to air on time with a very tight shirt, diabolical tie and Daryl Eastlake's blazer — a bit small but as I was sitting down, it didn't much matter.

Yes, airline travel is great . . . about the only thing we can be certain of is the cost and potential destination. Although even they sometimes can change!

Life in the Old Croc yet

'A DREADFUL LOOKING, SLIMY THING WITH A MOUTH FULL OF INCH-LONG TEETH'

It was during a fishing excurision down the Demerara River in Guyana that Doug Walters learned of Terry Jenner's phobias regarding crocodiles, piranha fish and the like.

As understandable as the aversion might be, it provided Walters with a chance to floor his room-mate and also (and much more importantly) his skipper Ian Chappell.

I just happened to be privy to the whole dastardly performance.

This was on the 1973 tour of the West Indies and at the end of the fourth Test match at Georgetown, Guyana, Doug said he'd like to go fishing. So he quickly organised someone to set up a day on the Demerara River.

The best way I could describe the boat is that it was 'no more than a long dug out log'.

The Geelong antique dealer and our opening batsman, Ian Redpath, was at the front or bow of the 'log'. And every little wave the floating log passed over sent Redders' Adam's apple crashing into the underside of his very angluar jaw bone.

Naturally the centre position was occupied by Dougie himself and bringing up the rear was leg spinner Terry Jenner, from South Australia.

TJ, as he was known to his team-mates, just happened to have a can of beer in one hand, the other was dangling over the edge into the brown, muddy water.

Behind him stood an enormous Guyanese man who must have been six foot six inches tall and had muscles growing out of muscles. He was poling the log along and also acted as our guide for the day.

After a short while he shouted in Jenner's ear: "I wouldn't leave dem dere fingers in dat dere water mate!!!"

"Why?" asked TJ.

"Cause dem dere piranhas really love dat white meat man!!!"

Naturally, this caused Jenner's right hand to be pulled quickly out of the rapid-flowing river.

"I suppose you've got crocodiles and alligators over here too, mate?" asked Jenner.

Silenced reigned supreme for a moment, then the big black man spoke, "What do you think dat is over dere — a block of flats?" Just as a 12-foot long greasy alligator opened up its jaws and yawned. Quick as a flash it slid through the mud at the water's edge and into the river.

At this stage the lads didn't want to fish any more — in fact they were beginning to sober up very smartly. Then, the man with the pole in his hand, shouted: "Look out boys. If those three hippopotamuses yawn and we crash into dem, we'ez dead. We really are!!!"

I need not say what happened. That gnarled log headed straight back to shore and not one of the lines had been dampened.

Later, Dougie mentioned that he'd love a stuffed crocodile to take back home to Australia. He reckoned it would look tremendous sitting on top of his TV set — just below the flying ducks — and fitted with a couple of cat's eye marbles for eyes.

He got one and christened it 'Inchan', after the left-arm spin bowler from Trinidad named Inchan Ali . . . and was determined to have some fun before it got to the taxidermist.

The crocodile he had been given was about four foot long, a dreadful looking, slimy thing with a mouth full of inch-long teeth.

His room-mate, TJ, had had a truck load of rum and coke on the fateful night and was hooking yorkers when he finally came in.

We were staying at a hotel in Georgetown that was rated as five stars. Honestly, they were pretty dim stars.

About eleven o'clock that night, while TJ was out, Dougie short-sheeted his bed and in between the crisp white sheets was placed Inchan, the crocodile.

As you can imagine, as soon as TJ eventually made it to bed, and I might add, not wearing a stitch of clothing. He sat bolt upright. Now the inside of the thigh is fairly sensitive and the deeper he slid into the bed the closer the teeth got to the action.

He had sobered up in seconds and was obviously terrified, Doug and I just happened to be in the wardrobe at the time.

TJ refused to sleep in the same room as Dougie Walters for the next two nights. It really did shake the lad up badly.

The boy from Dungog had struck again!

Despite his efforts on TJ, Doug's crowning glory was to get his captain at the time, Ian Chappell. It took him 10 years to get him and he *really* got him with Inchan.

Chappelli and Walters had organised a game of golf at Royal Georgetown, Guyana. It is an unbelievable golf course — the caddies wear Dunlop rubbers, size 12, made in India, with enormous hammer head toes extending from each shoe.

The lurk is to pick up the golf ball between the big toe and the second toe, if it is positioned in a bad lie, then walk 50 metres down the fairway shouting, "Gee boss lovely lie right here", pointing to the end of their shoes.

Dougie knew that Chappelli would wear his favorite golf clothes; those diabolical red and white, checked trousers that he so often wore. I'm sure they must have been a table cloth before they were stitched up.

Chappelli left the strides folded neatly over the back of a chair in his room and then went to breakfast — casually dressed in shorts. That was the moment Dougie had waited for. While his captain was at brekkie, Dougie grabbed the master key by bribing the girl at the front desk with a couple of tickets to the next cricket match, and gained access to the room.

He then carefully placed the crocodile with the big teeth into the crutch of the trousers and waited. Doug stood outside the room to force Chappelli to hastily put on the trousers. Walters was convulsed with laughter when the contact was made with Inchan, the crocodile.

Needless to say, Chappelli had screamed, jumped about and succeeded only in ripping the crutch out of beloved golf pants. He fell to the floor entangled in a mass of shredded material as Inchan fell limp under the bed.

All that could be seen was this magnificent set of crocodile teeth smiling from the floor at Chappelli's hairy legs.

Dougie couldn't believe his good fortune, although he lost a little of his enthusiasm when Chappelli suggested that it would be very unwise for him to sleep heavily.

He rather emphatically told Dougie: "I'll get you, somewhere, some place, at some time. It might not be this trip or even this year, but I promise I'll get you."

Sharing a bet with a mate
'AT TIMES THE SPINNING WHEEL APPEARED HYPNOTIC'

How could anyone resist odds of 500 to one in a two horse race? Or should I say in a cricket match. It is now common knowledge that two of Australia's former greats, Dennis Lillee and Rodney Marsh successfully combined their talents and vast experience to wager a little bet during the fateful 1981 official tour of England. Kim Hughes was the captain of the team — Australia lost the Ashes 3-1 after winning the first Test match.

At cricket grounds everywhere in England, the very large betting firm Ladbrokes have their colourful tents strategically placed. Inside, it is possible to have a bet on anything from a win or loss, to which batsman scores the first century in the game, or even how many wickets will fall in the first session of play. Incredible as it may seem they get many takers.

In the third Test of the '81 series at Headingley, Leeds, where England were forced to follow on, England's chances of a win at this stage of the contest were rated at 500 to one. The great bowler/wicket keeper combination couldn't resist the urge to have a wee punt.

It was the turning point, after a run of outs in the Test career of all-rounder Ian Botham, the then deposed captain. *Wisden,* the cricket almanac, shows the barrel-chested Englishman won the next Test match almost single handedly with a belligerent 149 runs not out.

It is difficult to describe how the two champion Australian cricketers must have felt after losing the encounter from that position, but also after winning a substantial amount of money because of it — Catch 22, eh?

My mate Dougie Walters didn't get selected for that tour despite a brilliant domestic season. On top of that disappointment, his two former team-mates, who knew of his penchant for a bet didn't even contact him. As Dougie said later, "You don't get odds like that very often, and what are mates for, if you can't share a good bet?" He's still pretty dirty on those two!

Cricketers have been betting in one form or another for many years. My first visit to a casino occurred during the 1975 tour of England. Before that there had been rumours of some members of the 1973 touring party in the Caribbean losing heaps at the island paradise gambling house.

It may have been the accountancy background of Western Australian Ross Edwards that consistently lured him to the roulette table to watch the small white marble roll.

Antigua must be one of the most beautiful islands on earth, yet tiny as it is, there was even a casino to be found there. Unfortunately for 'Rosco' he didn't realise the place was almost certainly 'managed' by a mafia-type element on the duty free island, until he returned home — and more than a little out of pocket. This type of learning experience can be very painful and obviously costly. Ask Ross!

In 1975 it was no surprise to see Ross regularly in the first cab alongside Rod Marsh, Richie Robinson and myself, destined for the Sportsman's Club. This was a very famous and expensive gaming house frequented by anyone from rich Arabs to crazy sporting personalities like us.

The rather sombre exterior of the building, located right in the centre of London, gave way to a very plush chandeliered and carpeted expanse, set off by very sensitive mood lighting, except of course for the bright lights focused on the gaming tables themselves.

I don't have to say how impressed our lads were by the croupiers — beautifully dressed in brilliant red, clinging material. In all cases the girls appeared to have most of their dress fronts missing. Necklines regularly plunged to the navel — and nice navels at that.

I can't really remember what colour eyes they had, and Thommo, another regular customer, often worried about most of them getting a chill in the region of the ribs — you know English weather and all that stuff! He's really a very caring guy Jeff Thomson, except if you're an England batsman!

It was during one of many nights spent at the Sportsman's Club that the unexpected happened!

About half a dozen cricketers were just enjoying the wonderful food in the restaurant over a couple of drinks and a few yarns when . . . Baaang! Boooom! Craaash! . . . the thundering noise of an explosion gate-crashed our well settled 'table for six' and every other table too!

The three-storey building shook violently. Glass droplets from the swaying chandeliers fell from above like huge diamonds out of the sky. The look of fear soon replaced that of frivolity . . . four of the six players promptly left the table, both for safety reasons and also to find out what was going on. Was it an IRA bomb?

Only Thommo and myself remained. Our theory was if we were going to go we might as well go on a full stomach. I can still see Thommo leaning across the table stabbing two or three quarter-eaten steaks off his mates' plates. "What do you think, Tang? Not bloody bad, eh?"

I had to agree — no matter how much money we lost that night we got our money's worth!

Later that evening the others returned to the table only to find their plates empty. It was learned that in fact an IRA bomb had exploded, completely demolishing the shop front of the business right next door to the casino. Chaos everywhere as police and security guys swarmed into the club.

Some weeks later, Rodney Marsh took me into his confidence and invited little old Tangles to be his betting partner for the night — I agreed without hesitation. To then I was purely an odds or evens, black or red, fifty percent chance of winning gambler. But with new horizons to be challenged, I thought, why not.

The little wicket keeper with the billiard table legs was riding a winning streak at the time — I felt like I couldn't lose. Silly boy!

Roulette was to be our game and £20 each was our initial stake. We should have got off to a good start with £40 worth of £1 chips — anyway the piles looked very impressive on the rich green felt table top. What next?

Normally the more astute gamblers like Richie Robinson and Ross Edwards would spend hour after hour carefully documenting the numbers as they came up looking for a significant pattern of numbers to emerge. No such strategy with Marshie — he just barged straight in with a handful of chips. I wasn't even asked what my favourite numbers were.

Five times in less than five minutes he placed our chips rather haphazardly on any of the 36 numbers on the table — I still hadn't been consulted, we weren't winning and my palms had become very sweaty! The moment I'd dreaded. No chips left. I was not impressed. He than asked me for another £20 and I was stupid enough to give it to him.

Immediately our stocks looked good again, 40 £1 chips nestled in Rodney's meaty palm. I thought: "Strewth he's not even going to put these down on the table."

My pockets seemed unusually empty. Already our free meal was looking like costing £40 —a bit steep!

Talk about the marble rolling loudly around the circular tray of numbers in front of the glamorous young woman. At times the spinning wheel appeared hypnotic, but inside my head the marbles were really rolling around. I came rapidly to the conclusion at the rate of losing £4 a minute, it wasn't going to take that long to lose the entire tour allowance of $2700 for the five months stay.

Commonsense should have prevailed when he asked me for another £10 . . . but it didn't! Greed took over. I had visions of him winning a heap of money on the next spin and not wanting to share it with me because I had no guts to continue . . . and he still hadn't looked like giving me a drop on any of the numbers I wanted. Very inconsiderate indeed.

Gee, we looked the part . . . pure wool sportscoats, clean shaven, collar and tie. In many ways the image of a couple of punters without any money. If we continued our poor form, no chips either.

We had not been playing, sorry, Rodney had not been playing anymore than a quarter of an hour and we were both 50 quid in the red — bloody unreal! What was going on?

We had only two solitary chips left. He looked at me with a cheeky smirk. "Let's go for broke, eh?." Go for broke, with two pounds! Again I agreed and then he placed one chip directly on top of the other — they covered No. 35 completely.

Then I questioned him. "Why bloody 35? What's so special about 35?" He quickly chuckled at me. "Cause it's a lucky number, pal! Believe me this is the one!" Why did he leave it this long to put 'our' money on the lucky one?

All bets placed, and the little white ball rolled quickly around the perimeter of the blurred circle of black and red numbers. It seemed like an eternity until the marble came to rest — yes, on No. 35. We were back in town.

Two chips at 35 to 1 meant a winning of £70. As the chips were pushed across the table in our direction, I could feel my heart beat a bit faster. This charged sensation is probably what all the big gamblers thrive on — the uncertainty of the dice or wheel!

Just metres away Arabs were playing for enormous quantities of money with £1000 chips. One fella must have had £50,000 on the table in front of him — these were gold rectangles and not the coloured circular discs that we now owned. Before leaving the club we witnessed the same gambler lose £20,000 in 10 minutes — I felt sick!

But that was another table, another lifestyle thank goodness. Perhaps I should have batted more like I gambled — with caution, for 50 of those little chips bulged from my coat pocket. 'Bacchus' Marsh my team-mate and gambling partner continued our strategy in earnest. Placing more chips all over the table, 10 or 12 at a time.

We were lucky this time! Eventually when we did walk away from the bright lights of the tables and that hazy, smoke-filled room, our profit for the night was £140 each. You little beauty! Once was enough for me.

I found it an unnecessary and gut-wrenching experience. I can now understand how people lose lots of money and sometimes everything they own.

By 1977 Rodney Marsh was a veteran gambler with a notorious amount of success. So it came as no surprise, after winning our first game at Arundel Castle against the Duchess of Norfolk's XI, that we invested our £400 winnings.

How could we invest £400 in England? Give it to big bad Rodney Marsh to treble at the casino — a unanimous decision.

On that occasion he not only lost our £400 but also £600 of his own trying to get it back. You can't beat bad luck, eh? Never again!

I should mention that over my two trips to England 'Bacchus' did extremely well. Except for the night I lost eight or nine £5 chips back against a run of three odds. In other words I placed my money on the evens with a good chance of winning after seeing three consecutive odd numbers turn up. I ran out of money after 12 consecutive odds had come up and I just had to tell somebody.

As usual Rodney Marsh was nearby and took up where I left off. Incredibly it went to 19 straight odds and Rodney went in heavily, £20 a spin. Which meant every time he lost, he had to double his stake just to get his money back. So £20, £40, £80, £160 . . . and so on. He wished I had never opened my mouth that night!

But as Dougie Walters said, "What are mates for if they can't share a bet?"

Introduction to a fiery wicket
'THEN THEY HIT US WITH THEIR SECRET WEAPON'

Even as a little boy, my dad told me not to accept lifts from strangers, no matter how many lollies they offered. Nevertheless, I accepted an offer from John Maley — the man who gained fame for producing those magnificent artificial wickets for World Series Cricket in Australia — to accompany him on an unofficial sight-seeing tour of Jamaica during the 1979 World Series tour of the Caribbean.

The photographic angle appealed to me.

John had hired a local cab driver to take us, and even at $25 a head, it appeared to be a worthwhile exercise.

The only problem was that it was taking something of a chance with a cab driver about whom we knew nothing at all, on an island not known for its political stability.

But Maley was adamant that the trip would be an experience never to forget.

Next day, the driver turned up with a 1952 Chevrolet that looked is if it would need a tanker to follow, just to keep it in petrol. The $50 we paid him would have brought that heap of metal three times over.

The driver looked the part with a big, baggy, red velvet golf cap. From the way he leaned out of the window to greet everyone he saw he obviously knew all the population of Kingston.

Our first stop came when the driver said he had to make a call to his home deep in the backblocks of the city where very few white people ever go.

As he went inside, we cringed, certain that he was about to get a gun, kill us and take our money. Our bodies never would be found, our imaginations went wild!

Our worries were needless as our chauffeur returned and we set off through the black slum at incredible speed. I pushed the 'third' lens out the window and began snapping away happily.

Photographers, especially white ones, were not particularly liked in that area, fists were aimed, people screamed obscenities, and I fancy a couple

151

of bricks were thrown in our direction. But we were safe while the driver kept his accelerator pedal flat to the floor. I don't think he knew any other way to drive.

Soon we were out in the country leading to the hills. Again John Maley and I started wondering about the wisdom of this trip, as we seemed to be a long way from the centre of civilisation and too young to die.

Eventually we pulled up at a crudely constructed shanty — four corner posts and a few big leaves thrown over the frame work for a roof, to give a bit of shade from the sun. But I doubt if it would have kept rain out.

Hanging from the roof was an enormous cooking pot, with a fire blazing away underneath — the centre piece for cannibal cartoons.

The cabby decided that it was time to eat and while he chatted to two locals in their own patois, we chose what we wanted. We picked some huge bananas, some custard fruit and a couple of corn cobs from the cooking pot, as well as some of the local apples. They really were delicious, something between a water melon and a snow apple with no pips in the middle.

I think the lot cost us about 50 cents and the driver got his for nothing in return for bringing in the trade.

With some effort, we ate our huge lunch and then drove to a place called Achios Rios — very beautiful and very popular with American tourists.

After a swim and a run along the beach, we headed off to the more remote parts of the Jamaican outback. He had an unusual technique, that driver. We rarely seemed to go at less than 100 miles an hour, with one hand on the wheel, one hand gripping a banana and his head swivelling around talking to us most of the time.

Once Maley called out "please stop, go back." The driver obliged by putting the machine straight into reverse, without stopping. We suddenly seemed to be going 50 miles an hour backwards. After I scraped myself off the windscreen — no safety belts in Jamaica — I chanced on what had caught John's eye. It wa a tiny patch of brown on which men were trying to prepare a cricket pitch.

I suppose the ground was the size of many of those used in Melbourne for minor competitions, the difference was that it was cut into the side of a hill and ringed with palm trees, except the members end, which dropped sheer for a thousand feet or so into the sea. A good straight hit there would have seen the batsman score six.

Maley, whose interest in the preparation of cricket wickets borders on the fanatical, gained a world-wide reputation for making all the pitches for World Series Cricket matches in Australia during the cricket revolution between 1977 and 1979.

The looks we got as we started to walk towards the men were not very inviting.

I was all for beating a hasty retreat, but John would have none of that. We got about half-way when two of the fellows came to meet us. Suddenly it became obvious that they recognised me — though they had no television in that part of the world.

Feeling more confident, I introduced him to Mr Maley and told him that he was a man who had made the Packer wickets — Kerry Packer's right hand man. I thought I was witnessing the second coming. They had a problem and would Mr Maley care to help them sort it out. Of course he would.

The problem was that it had rained there recently. One of those tropical downpours that deposits large amounts of water in a short space of time.

There might have been four blades of grass on the whole wicket area, the rest was clay and mud. The team had a roller that looked as if it had started life as a 44-gallon drum, and when they used it it just picked up the mud and made more of a mess.

Being resourceful, they had gotten over the problems by placing an old Air Force mattress over the area and rolling over the top of it bit by bit.

The pitch had a bit of a dog-back in it but it was better than no pitch at all.

Despite their work it was obvious to John and me that play could not start on the pitch for about three days. Yet they told us solemnly that a match was scheduled to be played there at 4.30 p.m. that afternoon!

We discussed the technical difficulties of the situation and then they hit us with their secret weapon.

Having prepared the ground to their satisfaction, they drowned it with petrol and set it alight. Within 20 minutes the wicket was rock hard! I've heard stories about wickets being prepared like that in Pakistan and South Africa but never would I have believed it. It was one of the highlights of the tour for both of us and it is no doubt that one day those blokes will be telling their grandchildren how they met Johnny Maley and Max Walker on the local village green. If green can ever be the right word for it.

On the way back to Kingston, we stopped at what would be known in the Australian idiom as a bush pub. It had a dirt floor and not much else and the lighting was so bad that it was hard to tell us from the locals.

Again we used the driver as our passport for making sure there was no trouble. But we didn't have any worries. We hardly had ordered our first orange juice when an enormous man-mountain recognised me. From then on everything was on the house.

We had to shake hands with everybody at least half a dozen times and tell them what it was like to play with Lillee and the chaps. I don't think I would have bothered to describe the West Indies as anything else but great in that place. The customers in that pub were a great bunch: laborers, farmworkers, mechanics, just ordinary working people, the same as I'd known in Tasmania as a lad.

Out there in the country we did not have the same trouble as in downtown Kingston. They accepted us as we were. A different colour of our skin was just a curiosity.

That time, cricket again proved itself a great way of communicating in what might have been a very tense situation — people from two entirely different worlds coming together, enjoying each other's company.

I wish there was some way that all people could learn to get on together like that. We got back to our hotel safely, even though our driver had, perhaps, a little too much of that bush pub. When they turned on the free stuff for us, I fancy he thought all his Christmases had come at once.

Just call me Dennis . . .
'WE THOUGHT WE'D HIT THE BIG TIME'

John Newcombe's unmistakable bushy moustache is insured for more than a million dollars and is graphically represented on Newk's advertising and marketing logo. Dennis Lillee still sports a mean looking Mexican style droopy moustache — symbolic of perhaps the most recognisable head in Australian sport for more than a decade.

And me . . . well I've got a moustache too! I originally grew it to keep my very sensitive upper lip from painfully cracking under the heat of our blazing Aussie sun during a long day chasing a cricket ball all over the field.

Much to my amazement too, I discovered that the wiry growth was very effective in keeping the odd fly out of the corner of my mouth . . . even better than Aerogard!

I should add that I did grow mine well before D.K. Lillee agreed with my philosophy about moustaches.

I've no doubt that the game of cricket and a common droopy moustache was the reason so many people have asked me if my name's Dennis Lillee . . . I often say to them, "No he's got a better bowling action but then I'm better looking!" It gets varying reactions.

Nevertheless, it has got its advantages, even if I don't look anything like my mate at all. I've never been one to let an opportunity slip by whatever it may be . . . and they can occur in the most unlikely situations.

It was a few years back now, I was travelling alone to Adelaide from Melbourne to speak at a dinner there, and there were three people sitting in the row in front of me.

The hospitality on the commercial flight was great as usual. But I guessed by the loud laughter and chatter in front, that the hospitality may have began well before they boarded the plane. I was right too!

Finally, the well-manicured blonde woman in front, turned to me and asked the usual question, "Are you Dennis Lillee?"

I thought just for once I'll go along with this mob . . . I may even get a free glass of champagne. Before long we were all the best of mates — the middle-aged woman and her two male real-estate agent companions. They were celebrating the successful sale of a multi-million dollar property.

Having got a bit of a sniff of all this, I thought that I might soon need to blow my D.K. Lillee 'cover' if I was to use this chance meeting to advantage.

In no time at all my friends were attempting to flog me a penthouse apartment on the Gold Coast for a mere $500,000 complete with kidney-shaped swimming pool and 180 degree oceanic view. What a magnificent pad, but they were trying the wrong guy!

I cranked 'em up a little bit by giving their glossy, embossed colour brochure my undivided attention. Then, like the Three Stooges, they simultaneously greeted me with three identical over-sized, coin-shaped gold business cards with a raised $ sign in the middle ... names and details on the back. Just the look of these cards made me nervous and jumpy. But being young and gullible, I thought I'd give it a try.

So I said with authority in my voice, and that was hard for a man of so few years in this big bad world we live in, "What you really need is a decent architect, then you would have something to sell!" They looked shocked at my comment about their beautifully designed apartments. The threesome were attempting to sell units 'off-the-plan' for a five or 10 per cent deposit in advance. The principle worked in the boom years of the 70s with big profits being made, but many people got their fingers burnt later on in the 80s when they could no longer 'sell on' their 10 per cent 'investment'. They lost it all.

Also some of the big developers on the coast had enormous trouble unloading their still vacant high-rise apartments buildings — pigeon holes for retired people.

You might ask what's an ex-medium pace bowler doing raving on about these high rise buildings and real-estate. Well, I'm an architect by profession and I played cricket for fun.

I said, "You're not going to believe this but I'm not Dennis Lillee. Anyway you couldn't be luckier because I'm his mate Maxie Walker and I just happened to be an architect — now what more could you want?"

They were speechless ... but not for long! I picked their brains and they picked mine. We exchanged our business cards with a view to mutual benefit at a later date. I thought it was a case of file away under miscellaneous and useless. But stranger things have happened.

All the gold dust I laid on them must have worked because we did meet again, some weeks later. My partner Des Bloink and I had a meeting with the woman to show off a portfolio of our work skills and various expertise. I think we impressed her, but nothing happened for about six months.

Until one Friday night I received a frantic phone call saying she was in town and desperate for a schematic-design! Her Asian client had rejected the 15 previous designs for a nine-storey apartment building and was going home — she needed help! My partner and I worked day and night till Sunday morning — our deadline.

We met with her client and two friends. It turned out to be a very fruitful meeting. They loved our design and we were tentatively engaged. Thanks for the job Dennis!"

Within no time, days in fact, Des and I got off the aeroplane at the old

Coolangatta Airport. We were to be met by a syndicate representative from Surfers Paradise.

Des and I had only been in partnership less than 12 months. We thought we'd hit the big time . . . multi-storey development and good fees. Wow, at last it was all happening for us.

We were both too excited to see past our noses . . . I remember standing on the footpath outside the airport with an Adidas bag in hand containing a clean pair of underpants, toiletries plus a few shirts and most importantly the necessary pencils and paper to begin our project.

The two of us must have looked anything but a couple of whiz-kid architects from the south. Never let looks fool you, we knew we were good and capable of doing a professional job, we just couldn't afford the Christian Dior suits and all-leather carry bags.

After 10 minutes of waiting I said to Des, "Mate we've been sold the dummy!"

And it certainly looked that way. I jokingly pointed to a huge elongated black Cadillac parked over the road and said, "That's got to be us . . . The one with the chauffeur!"

Don't laugh — a small, olive-skinned man dressed in an immaculate black suit, white silk shirt, open right to the navel, and enough gold chains around his neck and wrist to open up a jewellery shop, slammed the car door and walked towards us! I quietly mentioned to Des, "I told you so!"

With a nervous laugh and a tickle in the throat, we made contact with our man and hopped into the back seat — it could have been straight out of *The Godfather.* Bloody unreal!

To quickly get to the moral of the story — he and his syndicate mates wined and dined us at the best restaurants during the evening and during the day we toiled hard . . . looking at the site, talking to the council, discussing our brief . . . dreaming of the future work we would get.

Does it sound good? In fact too good! They screwed us down on our fees with fast-talking and hospitality. We kept saying that we had to start somewhere — why not here! Being Melbourne-based wouldn't be a problem we mused. It's true that we all learn from experience . . . in our case a very costly one, almost crippling in its effect on us both.

Today we are still owed many thousands of dollars for our work . . . we were paid just enough to keep us interested and the drawings were completed, approved by council and accepted by the Asian client's representative. Herein lies the problem — our fast talking Australian-based representative, or co-ordinator for the Asian syndicate members, has flown the coop! And on everyone!

The striking nine-storey building, costing $1.8 million, is standing in all its glory on the Gold Coast but the architects', engineers' and other consultants' fees — $178,000 in all — are still outstanding. We were all caught napping and learnt the most painful way of all, through our hip pockets.

From Des and myself and our office he raped thousands of unpaid man hours, but we did pick up the receipt and it won't happen again.

And it certainly pays to check on who you have business dealings with of that magnitude, because the world is full of sharks, particularly in the building industry. Beware!!!

A Walk Down Memory Aisle

'THE USUALLY COMPOSED YOUNG WOMAN WAS LOOKING A BIT GREEN'

Doug Walters and I had just successfully passed the scrutiny of two Australian customs officers at Mascot International Airport, Sydney, after collecting yet another stamp in our small blue passports.

Two pimply-faced young policemen observing the X-ray baggage surveillance machine had a keen eye for faces. As Doug and I retrieved our briefcases and suit carriers from the scanner one of them quipped: "Where are you blokes off to? South Africa I suppose."

This was the time of the rebel tour controversy in early 1985. Doug removed the cigarette from the corner of his mouth and replied, "I felt a bit out of it actually, I haven't even been bloody well asked."

No, we weren't off to join the rebels on a tour of South Africa. We were off to New Zealand, the land of the long grey cloud. We were on a business trip to promote Indoor Cricket Arenas who were expanding into both New Zealand and England.

The thought of yet another international flight excited me as we quickly assessed the last-minute duty free shopping — as expected it wasn't long before Dougie asked me would I carry a 'spare' carton of cigarettes through the gate for him at the other end. What could I say?

I'm no Lord Snowdon with the camera but I do love photography . . . Doug doesn't. Needless to say, I was left to make a purchase in the camera shop on my own!

Dougie and our manager for the trip, Mr Tony Page, a director from Indoor Cricket Arenas, had in fact boarded the plane without me . . . very inconsiderate, especially as I was helping them with their cigarettes.

All my life I seem to have been batting at No. 11 or last. In fact in 1975 at Lord's, I was the last Australian player to meet the Queen. And now, judging by the impassioned plea for, "Mr Walker to please go immediately to gate 7" over the public address system — I was certain to be the last again to board the Air New Zealand jumbo. Yes, they were waiting on just one person — me.

I was unlucky in the seating arrangements, too. We were sitting upstairs in the last row of business class in a smoking area and I unfortunately had a notorious chain smoker on my left — Doug.

This was serious because I had very vivid memories of a long flight to England in 1975. On that occasion I had Jeff Thomson on one side of me and the boy from Dungog, Walters, on the other. It was like being sentenced to 28 hours of irritatiion. They enjoyed every minute of it, too.

I hate playing cards and before the big jet had even levelled out, down came my tray table to use for their continuous game of '500'. That wasn't too bad, but then 15 minutes after takeoff the poor hostess was summoned to begin supplying what seemed to me a never-ending supply of beer. With the help of some of their team-mates they drank the plane dry by Singapore, where new stocks of beer were taken on aboard. On top of that, they purposely directed all their filthy, blue-grey haze straight at me and with great accuracy — they loved doing it.

I tried not to over-react, but long before Singapore my eyes began to water and I'm certain I developed their smoker's cough. Not bad for somebody who hadn't had a puff.

Meanwhile, Garry Gilmour, the former Australian all rounder, was improving daily as Doug's understudy in the practical joker's stakes. He'd just handed the young and very pretty Qantas hostess a waxed paper sick bag about one third full. She gingerly accepted the parcel and immediately disposed of it at the rear of the plane. Moments later the young, uniformed lady returned with a cold face washer for Gus's forehead. By this time his seat was laid right back and the plot was set.

Most of the players sitting nearby were told the prank before Gus asked his female friend for a dessertspoon. She was surprised by his request but, as service is paramount, she was soon at his side with a lonely-looking dessertspoon. Gilmour's eyes had begun to light up with anticipation. So, too, had the interest of other passengers.

Without batting an eyelid, Gus sat upright in his chair — his expression was perfect, emotionless to say the least. From the floor between his legs he produced another white sick bag, about half full. He offered the bag to the hostess who wasn't impressed. Then the fun began, "Hang on lady!" he said.

Gilmour gently took the bulging paper bag from the girl's grip and proceeded to open it up. It looked like he might be violently ill again, but not our Gus. At this stage all eyes focussed on either the sick bag or the brown-eyed hostie. There was a strange silence in the air.

With the stainless steel spoon held tightly in his left hand, he delved deep into the bag, at the same time bringing his chin down towards the opening of the packet. By the time he had shovelled two spoonsful into his mouth, the usually very composed young woman was looking a bit green.

Gus smiled and offered the hostess a spoonful for herself, just as a small trickle of saliva dribbled down from the corner of his mouth to the extremities of his rather chisel-shaped chin. The expression on the Qantas staff member's face was expected . . . one of revulsion.

Everyone except the young lady knew what appeared to be a bag full of vomit was only a bag full of fruit salad.

Our airline attendant didn't appear to have the same sense of humour as everyone else. The laughter was loud and pointed, especially when she nearly tripped on some fresh 'dog's droppings' placed on the floor by Ross Edwards. It was a first go for 'Roscoe' and his plastic imitation — he was pleased with the result. I thought the beer might suddenly dry up after this, but no, it just kept coming down the aisle of the plane, tray after tray.

For the statisticians I think by his own admission Rodney Marsh holds the beer drinking record for a Sydney to London flight. That remains at 46 cans. No wonder he went through customs and immigration on a motorised buggy.

As the journey to NZ continued and lunch was served, we both walked down memory lane. Tony Page was lucky for he was sitting across the aisle where he got some paperwork done.

Doug was quick to remind me of the 1974 tour of NZ when after an internal flight, my suit carrier with all my suits, blazer and trousers failed to turn up with the other baggage.

Remember at 6'4" I'm a pretty hard guy to fit at the best of times. Expecially when there was only two hours to get organised for the mayoral reception at the Wellington Civic Centre.

It was most embarrassing walking up the steps to the civic centre entrance in Keith Stackpole's trousers and brown sports coat. The gear fitted beautifully — around the waist, but from the top of my shoes to the bottom of my trousers must have been a gap of 3½ inches and my dark coloured socks didn't match, but what could I do?

The problems incurred in the arms were similar. My left arm continually displayed my watch. I must have looked like a gorilla. Gee, that coat was tight under the armpits, and the crutch of the trousers . . . well I almost talked in a high-pitched voice.

It took some three days to locate my suit carrier — in Dunedin. Luckily I had my cricket gear in a separate case, or coffin, as we call the cumbersome box containers used for transporting all of the cricket gear necessary to fill a player's requirements on tour.

Back to 1985. On this trip Tony and Dougie had decided to bring their own golf sticks. That was fine until filling out the form for customs and immigration clearance to New Zealand. The bit about sporting equipment caused the problem — soil on his golf shoes.

At least Doug was honest enough and owned up to having dirty golf shoes. You should have seen 'em. Even taking into account his last game was played in the wet, they appeared to have half the Royal Melbourne golf course fairway still locked on to the sole. It must have been half an inch thick in places. Let's face it these customs inspectors aren't blind.

The result was that the shoes were impounded for quarantine reasons —maybe footrot or tinea, eh? Twenty minutes later the inspector returned to us with a plastic bag filled with heavy condensation. The bag contained two well-washed golfing shoes.

Doug's comment was, "What about the tops!" They only cleaned down the underneath part of each shoe to show off 20 sparkling metal sprigs. The basically white uppers were still filthy.

As Dougie said, "I suppose you could still get foot and mouth disease off the uppers". It did seem a bit strange though. Nevertheless at last we were at the Auckland International Airport —me with my new camera and Dougie with his extra carton of cigarettes.

He was actually pretty good company this time. It could have been worse.

Once, between Jamaica and Trinidad I sat in the very back row of a DC9 alongside a huge West Indian.

His name was Robert Smith — he didn't look like a Robert Smith. This fella must have been 23 stone judging by the amount of him that spilled over the arm rest between us and rested tightly against my ribs. His suntan was good and must have placed him in the area between 11.30 p.m. and midnight on the colour scale. He only had about four teeth left in both gums.

They say variety is the spice of life. I love people but this bloke was unreal. Talk about spicy. Every word he uttered was like a garlic-charged flame-thrower — remember he had me pinned firmly in the corner up against the window. His Bri-nylon shirt must have been the same one he'd been wearing for three or four days. It was really enhancing his body odour — a roll-on type deodorant would have helped this one.

The captain explained: "We've got a slight mechanical problem, please remain seated — we will only be a short while." I'd hate to be hanging by the neck for a short while. Two hours later we were still on the tarmac in sweltering conditions of about 40 degrees C and 95 per cent humidity. No air-conditioning, only the back and front doors of the aircraft open. They call it flow through ventilation.

By this time my friend and I had discussed quite a number of topics, generally with my face looking straight out of the window to avoid the shocking onslaught of this guy's breath . . .

Perspiration was freely flowing from Robert's forehead, down the sides of his face, and over the 10 or so corrugations in his enormous bull neck. Stains looking like Coca Cola were appearing on his shirt front and wherever else he perspired. It must have been big night out on the rum and coke for him! It did cross my mind that if he points to something through my window the stench from under his arms, coupled with his ghastly breath, will knock me out.

As we taxied down the long bitumen runway, I'd had enough, I just could not continue . . . but the plane was a full house. What could I do?

It was difficult and maybe even rude but I was desperate. I went to sleep half way through a sentence of his and remained that way until we touched down in Trinidad. At least it kept his mouth shut.

Dougie Walters was a dream compared to Robert Smith.